WHAT JESUS
WOULD SAY

WHAT JESUS WOULD SAY

TO: RUSH LIMBAUGH
MADONNA
BILL CLINTON
MICHAEL JORDAN
BART SIMPSON
DONALD TRUMP
MURPHY BROWN
MADALYN MURRAY O'HAIR
MOTHER TERESA
DAVID LETTERMAN

& You!

LEE STROBEL

ZondervanPublishingHouse
Grand Rapids, Michigan

A Division of HarperCollinsPublishers

Requests for information should be addressed to:
Zondervan Publishing House
Grand Rapids, Michigan 49530

Library of Congress Cataloging-in-Publication Data

Strobel, Lee Patrick.
    What Jesus would say : to Rush Limbaugh, Madonna, Bill Clinton, Michael
  Jordan, Bart Simpson, Mother Teresa, Donald Trump, Madalyn Murray O'Hair,
  David Letterman, Murphy Brown—and you / by Lee Strobel.
        p.   cm.
    ISBN 0-310-48511-8
    1. Christian life. 2. Celebrities—Conduct of life. 3. Jesus Christ—Political
and social views. 4. Jesus Christ—Counseling methods   I. Title.
BV4501.2.S817   1994
248—dc20   94–3698
                                                                CIP

Edited by John Sloan and Bea Sussman
Cover design by Paz Design Group
Interior design by Sue Vandenberg-Koppenol

94 95 96 97 98 99 00 01 02 /❖DH/ 10 9 8 7 6 5 4 3 2

To Leslie,
who has consistently shown me
how Jesus would treat others

Contents

Acknowledgments

I owe a sincere debt of thanks to several people who contributed to making this book a reality. As the introduction explains, Fred Vojtsek and Bill Hybels initiated the process, and I'm extremely grateful for their roles. My close friend and colleague Mark Mittelberg offered valuable input and editing, while the other member of my small group, Russ Robinson, provided excellent feedback and support. Garry Poole supplied encouragement and contributed to the David Letterman chapter. Brad Mitchell was a much appreciated sounding board. Laura Daughtry's upbeat attitude kept my spirits buoyed. Trevor Waldock helped by brainstorming the Madonna chapter with me. Jim Mellado of the Willow Creek Association, as well as John Raymond and John Sloan at Zondervan Publishing House, kept the project on target. And special thanks to my wife, Leslie, my daughter, Alison, and my son, Kyle, who kept me going when I thought I'd never finish.

Introduction

If you've ever participated in a brainstorming session, then you know that a lot of silly, outrageous ideas get brought up among the more serious ones. They're great for a laugh and to break the routine.

But as it turned out, it was one of those offbeat suggestions that eventually prompted the writing of this book.

You see, I was part of a meeting to discuss possible topics for Willow Creek Community Church's weekend services, which are designed to provide an introduction to the Christian faith.

This particular gathering happened to be taking place when Murphy Brown was the hottest subject in the country. The unwed pregnancy of this fictional TV newswoman became a front-page controversy after Vice President Dan Quayle criticized the program in his famous speech on family values.

"How's this for the title of a sermon?" staff member Fred Vojtsek called out during our meeting. "'What Jesus Would Say to Murphy Brown.'"

Everybody laughed, including Fred. It was a clever concept, but certainly too outlandish to actually use, right? We went on with more mainstream suggestions and forgot about Fred's tongue-in-cheek proposal.

But a week later, as I was struggling with what to explore during a series of upcoming messages, Senior Pastor Bill Hybels dropped by my office. "Why not pursue Fred's concept?" he suggested. "Why not talk about what Jesus might say to Murphy Brown?"

Come to think of it, why not? Certainly the Murphy Brown matter raised some important concerns—including family values and single parenthood—that were well worth examining from a biblical perspective. And based on accounts of what Jesus said to real-life people during His ministry, we do have some solid insights into what He might say to someone in her position today.

So I decided to try it, and the idea grew. In fact, I did two separate series of sermons in which I imagined what Jesus might say to such colorful and controversial figures as Madonna, Bart Simpson, Michael Jordan, Bill Clinton, and Mother Teresa. The messages opened up opportunities to look at success, leadership, prayer, skepticism, servanthood, and other important themes from a spiritual viewpoint.

Since the Murphy Brown message, other churches around the country have picked up the format and used it as a vehicle for discussing a wide variety of socially significant issues.

All of which has left Fred amused. "Hey," he said, "I was only kidding!"

What Jesus *Did* Say

Jesus was always saying the unexpected. Just when His followers thought they had Him figured out, He'd open His mouth and amaze them once more.

Jesus didn't kowtow to the smug religious leaders of the day. Instead, He challenged and criticized them with an authority and power that must have left their heads spinning. And He didn't look down on those relegated to the lower rungs of society. Rather, He was encouraging and sympathetic, treating them with dignity instead of disdain.

People were flabbergasted when He said they should love their enemies. They were aghast when He said to turn the other cheek when someone crossed them. They were intrigued by His parables and mesmerized by His description of God's kingdom. His listeners were awed by His wisdom, inspired by His morality, and melted by His love.

The Bible preserved Jesus' words so that people through-out the ages could apply them to their own lives. His messages are just as powerful, as stimulating, and as compassionate as they were when He originally delivered them.

Using the spirit and content of what Jesus taught, I've tried in this book to suggest what He might tell a whole range of well-known people today. But to head off possible misunderstandings, let me begin with a few caveats.

First, I'm sure that Jesus would have many things to say to each one of these individuals. However, I've generally chosen to zero in on particular topics that are especially appropriate for each person. For instance, I've focused on leadership in talking about Bill Clinton, on success with Donald Trump, and on servanthood with Mother Teresa. But I don't want to imply that these are the only areas Jesus would discuss with them.

Second, I don't have any supernatural revelations from God on what might be said to these people. These are merely my suggestions—based on the overall thrust of Jesus' teaching and on principles drawn from how He interacted with individuals in the pages of Scripture. You might think I'm off base in some cases, which is fine. Your insights may very well be better than mine. But if the book stimulates discussion on these critical topics and gets people thinking about Jesus' perspective, then I'll consider it worthwhile.

Third, I've tried to be sensitive to the people I'm profiling. Because I've never met them, I've had to rely on extensive research into their lives, and I've strived to give them the benefit of the doubt when there was ambiguity about their behavior or motives. I've attempted to write each chapter as if I were talking personally to them.

Fourth, I don't want this to be a finger-pointing exercise. Jesus would say a lot of things to you and me, too, and I've raised many of those matters throughout the book. We can all benefit greatly when we apply His teachings to our everyday lives.

With that out of the way, what do you think Jesus *would* say to Murphy Brown? Or to Madonna? Or, for that matter, to Rush Limbaugh and Donald Trump and Madalyn Murray O'Hair?

Well, read on. Let the conversations begin.

1

What Jesus Would Say to *Madonna*

Close your eyes and imagine a rock concert that goes beyond anything you've ever seen. Laser lights sweep the frenzied crowd. The music shrieks. And on stage there's erotic dancing and sexually explicit activity—not merely suggested, but actually being lived out like an X-rated movie come to life.

Imagine obscene, hate-filled language, and performers who humiliate each other with scorn and contempt. And then suppose that as the show concludes, some participants attack each other and commit murder right before your eyes. It would be a sickening scene of mayhem and carnage.

Madonna is criticized for *her* concerts, but compared with this fantasy, they would look like a Barney the Dinosaur video!

Where would such a terrifying spectacle originate? Consider the words of Jesus in Mark 7:21–22: "For from within, out of men's hearts, come evil thoughts, sexual immorality, theft, murder, adultery, greed, malice, deceit, lewdness, envy, slander, arrogance and folly."

My point is this: If we projected the hidden contents of the human heart onto a stage, we'd have a show that would sink to depths far lower than any Madonna concert. Think about your own secret desires, unspoken fantasies, and aggressive tendencies being brought to life for the whole world to see. I don't know about you, but I wouldn't want the shadows of my heart springing to life in front of a crowd.

I've started with this mental exercise because it would be easy for us to piously moralize about Madonna. And while I'm certainly not endorsing everything that goes on at her concerts, it's important to put matters into perspective at the outset by acknowledging the biblical truth that every one of us has some ugly stuff inside our hearts. The difference is that Madonna actually lives out some of her fantasies in a very suggestive way—which incenses many people and makes her an easy target for condemnation.

But Jesus doesn't want to be in the condemnation business; He prefers the human reclamation business. His favorite activity is reclaiming the lives of wayward people.

He demonstrated that when a woman caught in adultery was brought before Him, as described in John 8:3–11. While He did confront her wrongdoing by challenging her to stop her immoral activity, He also extended grace to her. And He warned the religious leaders against being too judgmental toward her without acknowledging that they, too, harbored secret sins.

And maybe He'd caution us along those same lines as we begin examining the modern phenomenon of Madonna Louise Veronica Ciccone.

A Doctorate in Street Smarts

Few celebrities have been more popular targets for criticism than Madonna—and, frankly, she loves it. Her favorite pastime, she says, is pushing people's outrage buttons. As one critic commented, "Giving her bad publicity is like trying to put out a fire with gasoline."

All of that publicity—both positive and negative—has propelled Madonna into becoming one of the wealthiest and most influential figures in current pop culture. While music critics agree that she's a decent singer, a good dancer, and a passable actress, where she *really* excels—in fact, where she's been declared a flat-out genius—is in packaging her image, marketing herself, and using the media. "Manipulating people," Madonna once said, "*that's* what I'm good at."

And it has paid off. Her photo has been emblazoned across the cover of *Forbes* magazine with the headline: "Amerca's Smartest Business Woman?" The article described her as a savvy promoter, owner of a half dozen companies with hundreds of employees, and the recipient of $125 million in earnings over a five-year period. *Time* magazine called her "a high school graduate with a doctorate in street smarts."

Her earning power is supercharged by her ongoing ability to generate controversy. For example, a few years ago Pepsi paid her $5 million to star in three commercials. But shortly after the first one aired, Madonna released a music video in which she danced seductively in front of a burning cross, and religious groups pressured Pepsi into abandoning her as a spokesperson. But still, she got to keep the $5 million!

Another time, she produced a video called *Justify My Love* that was too hot even for MTV to handle. The resulting controversy brought her millions of dollars in free publicity and landed her on *Nightline*, where host Forrest Sawyer commented that all of the hoopla would certainly boost sales of her video and album.

"In the end, you're going to wind up making even more money than you would have," he remarked.

"Yeah," she replied cheerily. "So, lucky me."

Her concerts only attracted more attention when Toronto police threatened to raid one of them and two others were canceled in Italy because of religious pressure. And the ruckus caused by the publication of her book *Sex*, with its sadomasochistic theme, helped it sell more than 800,000 copies at $50 each.

No wonder marketing experts consider her a master!

Desperately Seeking Something

If we focused on a one-word theme for this chapter about Madonna, it could very well be "manipulation." Or it could be "materialism," since she has billed herself as the Material Girl. Perhaps "sex" would be the word, since the self-professed Boy Toy has admittedly explored that topic quite a bit. Another alternative would be "ambition," as in her *Blonde Ambition* concert tour.

But at the risk of starting some controversy myself, the one-word theme I've selected is something you might not expect—it's "seeker." You see, I believe that in her own way, Madonna is desperately seeking *something* to give her life meaning.

She's seeking answers to her spiritual confusion; she's seeking acceptance; and she's seeking the fulfillment and happiness that have eluded her despite financial success. Interestingly, Mother Teresa spends her life trying to please God, and she says she's absolutely happy and fulfilled, whereas Madonna spends her life trying to please herself, and she says she doesn't know *anybody* who's happy.

I believe that Madonna—at least, to some degree, in her own way—is seeking God. I think there's a reason why she gathers her troupe into a hand-holding circle before each concert and takes time to pray. Sure, her prayers may be self-serving—sometimes merely a way to encourage or even lecture her entourage. But at other times she seems to be sincerely trying to connect with Someone.

In fact, consider for a moment if the same could be true for you. Maybe "seeker" isn't a label you would normally use for yourself, but think about the possibility that the things you've been chasing in your own life might be, in reality, a search for that missing puzzle piece of God that would complete your soul.

So as we explore what Jesus might say to Madonna, think about whether His words could apply to you as well, even though your life has been quite a bit different from hers.

God as He Isn't

While I'm sure there's a wide range of comments Jesus would make to Madonna, I'm going to propose three pairs of unexpected words that He might say. The first is simply, "I'm grieved."

You might suspect He would say this because of what she *does*, but I could picture Him uttering those words because of what was *done to* her. "Madonna," He might say, "I'm grieved that your childhood experience with religion left you with such a distorted and inaccurate impression of who I really am."

You see, like a lot of people, while Madonna was growing up, she developed a picture of God that bears scant resemblance to the God of the Bible. Regardless of whether this was because of the content of what she was taught or the way in which she was taught, the result is that she emerged with so many misunderstandings about God that it's no wonder she's spiritually befuddled.

She seems to have grown up seeing the God of Scripture as someone who demeans women, who doesn't tolerate questions, who enjoys heaping on guilt, who issues capricious and rigid rules—and who will always find *something* wrong whenever people are having fun. And that has colored the way she thinks of Him. You can see that in her music videos, with their brooding and almost sinister symbolism of God and the church.

Unfortunately many children are introduced to such a distortion of God that they end up rejecting Him—based on those misconceptions—without even knowing what He's really like. In fact, I know a Christian who says this to people who tell him that they've abandoned God: "Tell me about the God you don't believe in, because the chances are that I don't believe in that God either."

Maybe the picture you formed of God during your upbringing was that He's boring and irrelevant, or distant and unknowable, or eager to punish and squelch your fun, or unresponsive and powerless, or a master of guilt and shame. Your impression might be that God prefers rituals over relationships or that He demands blind, unthinking obedience.

That may not have been your denomination's teachings, but maybe it's how you envision God because that's the way He was modeled in your family or local congregation. And so you, like Madonna, have stayed away from church for a while. Perhaps you've stopped looking to God for solutions and now you're looking elsewhere—and yet you haven't found any answers that have satisfied your soul.

I think that would grieve Jesus deeply. The Bible cautions in Colossians 2:8: "Don't let others spoil your faith and joy with their philosophies, their wrong and shallow answers built on men's thoughts and ideas, instead of on what Christ has said" (LB).

God created His church so that men and women could communicate His message accurately through the ages and demonstrate the kind of loving and caring community He wants for His followers. Where people have remained faithful to His teachings, the church has become a magnet for spiritual seekers because they see a depth of relationships and fulfillment that other institutions in society can't match. But because churches are made up of people, and people are flawed, some teach an inaccurate view of God that repels seekers rather than attracts them.

Madonna has said, "I think the church pretty much stays with you so that whatever was drilled into you when you were growing up, whatever your picture of God was, I think you die with that image in your head."

But, fortunately, that doesn't have to be the case.

The Irresistible Jesus

The Bible says in Jeremiah 29:13 that if you sincerely seek the truth about God, then you will find it. And when you *do* get beyond the misconceptions and come to a more balanced understanding of who God is, you'll discover that He's awfully hard to resist.

He'll show you that He's not a God of shame. He wants to help you constructively face up to your wrongdoing so He can completely forgive you and remove the acid of guilt that can eat away at your life. Romans 8:1 declares, "Therefore, there is now no condemnation for those who are in Christ Jesus."

He's not a God who arbitrarily issues rules to undermine your enjoyment of life, but He lovingly offers you wise and sensible counsel to save you from ultimately hurting yourself and others. After all, He designed you—and so He knows best how you can maximize your life.

He's not a God who treats women as second-class citizens. A thorough study of Scripture shows that He created women as equal bearers of His image and has given them full freedom to develop the gifts and abilities He has implanted in them.

And He's not a God who demands blind, unthinking faith. When Jesus was asked in Mark 12:28 for God's most important command, He said it was not only to love God with all your heart, soul, and strength, but also with your *mind*. God wants us to be thinkers.

One troubling aspect of Madonna's early religious experience was that she had so many questions that apparently nobody was willing to answer. For instance, in *Truth or Dare*, a documentary about one of her concert tours, she is seen visiting the grave of her mother, who died when Madonna was only five years old.

"My mother's death was just a big mystery to me when I was a child, and no one really explained it," Madonna said. "She was really religious, so I never understood why she was taken away from us. It just seemed so unfair. I never thought that she had done something wrong, so oftentimes I'd wonder what *I'd* done wrong."

The church, of all places, should encourage people—especially children and teenagers—to process the deepest and most profound issues they are struggling with. The church shouldn't shun those with doubts; it should embrace them as they search for truth. I wish all spiritual seekers could imagine a big sign outside churches saying *Questions Welcome!*

You see, there is no sincere question in your mind that God wouldn't want you to ask. While we may not have complete answers this side of eternity, the Bible provides rich insights to help us get past the sticking points that stymie our spiritual journey. That's how misunderstandings about God are resolved.

Think about your own quest for God. Could it be that the problem between you and Him is that He's not really the God you were taught He is? I think that's true with Madonna. Or could it be that you gave up trying to connect with God because you were unable to see Him as a deity worth knowing? If that's true, what can you do?

One answer would be to go to someone who had firsthand knowledge about Jesus Christ—someone who knew Him personally, who witnessed His miracles, listened to His teachings, quizzed him about His parables, observed his character, experienced His compassion, and saw Him conquer the grave.

A person, for instance, like the apostle John. He has carefully recorded his experiences in the gospel bearing his name. He didn't report conjecture or speculation, but emphasized in 1 John 1:1 that he focused on what "we have seen with our eyes, which we have looked at and our hands have touched."

Why not pick up a Bible and spend some time reading his biography of Jesus? As you begin, try to set aside your preconceptions and prejudices, and let John introduce you to Jesus as He really is.

I think you'll find what I discovered when I began to investigate seriously the truth about Jesus: *To know Him is to love Him.* Actually, if your attitude is that you don't love Him, then it could be because you don't really know Him. You may know only an incomplete or distorted view of Jesus.

Frankly, I think Jesus would say to Madonna and you, "I'm grieved that your image of Me is so inaccurate. But now—let's do something about it. I've made sure that you've got a record of My life that carefully preserves a correct picture of Me. Read it, study it, immerse yourself in it—and you'll emerge with a fresh understanding of who I am."

What's Driving Madonna

I think the next pair of words from Jesus would be just as unanticipated as the first. I believe He would tell Madonna: "I understand." To a woman who's probably expecting to get slapped down by God, I think those words would grab Madonna's attention.

I could hear Jesus elaborate this way: "I understand, Madonna, how living a life without Me can cause you to seek fulfillment in other ways—including ways that are ultimately self-destructive and self-defeating. I've seen people fall into that trap time and time again. Believe me . . . I understand."

I think Jesus would look beyond Madonna's bawdy, headline-grabbing behavior and unearth the personal dynamics that are driving her to do what she does. After all, like each of us, her outward behavior is just a manifestation of what's going on inside.

And while I'm not saying that Jesus would blithely overlook her sinful actions—the Bible makes it clear that we'll all be held accountable for how we've lived our lives—I think He'd take the time to help her understand the forces that are driving her. Because, in the end, Jesus has the power to heal the inner source of pain that's provoking her outward conduct.

That's what Jesus did when He encountered a Samaritan woman at a well, as described in John 4:7–42. From His divine insight, Jesus knew that she had been divorced from five different husbands and that she was currently living a sexually immoral lifestyle with another man.

While He didn't excuse her behavior, Jesus did peer inside of her and diagnose how her misconduct was being driven by a spiritual void in her life. So He gave her the divine truth that she was thirsty for, knowing that as she grew in her understanding and love of God, it would eventually revolutionize the way she lived her life.

So what about Madonna—what inner dynamics are driving her outrageous behavior? "To use a technical psychiatric term," said one news magazine, "Madonna is a complicated nut." And although that's true, in reading through volumes of interviews with her I came across this very revealing quote in *Vogue* magazine:

> "I have an iron will," Madonna explained, "and all of my will has always been to conquer some horrible feeling of inadequacy. I'm always struggling with that fear. I push past one spell of it and discover myself as a special human being, and then I get to another stage and think I'm mediocre and uninteresting. And I find a way to get myself out of that again and again. My drive in life is from this horrible fear of being mediocre. That's always been pushing me, pushing me. Because even though I've become somebody, I still have to prove that I'm SOME-BODY. My struggle has never ended, and it probably never will."

You can see how that compulsion has played out in Madonna's life. Every couple of years she completely reshapes her persona, developing a new and more daring version of herself to market to the public. She's on a treadmill of having to do something more outrageous year after year to try to maintain the interest and admiration of her fans so she will feel worthwhile.

Psychologists say that our sense of personal worth is based on what we think the most important person in our life thinks about us. For Madonna, if seems like the most important people in her life are her fans, because they're the ones who affirm her value as an individual.

In a revealing scene during *Truth or Dare*, Madonna is shown praying with her fellow performers just before her concert in her hometown of Detroit. She asks God for a strong performance that evening, adding: "Even though it's not supposed to matter, it does matter what they think. So I ask You to give me that little extra something special to show everybody here that I did make something out of my life."

You see, she craves the affirmation of her fans to prove to herself that she's *somebody*. But what will happen to her sense of self-worth when her popularity begins to slip? As one psychologist has said, "She's in for a huge depression."

And there are signs of slippage. Her 1993 *Girlie Show* tour brought yawns from some critics, who said they're getting tired of Madonna constantly trying to reinvent herself. "Her attempts now to shock and titillate have become belabored self-parodies," wrote the *Washington Post's* Tom Shales. Said one newspaper headline: "Madonna's 'Girlie Show' Is Silly, Not Shocking."

The Jesus Alternative

But think about this: What would happen if Madonna were to come to an accurate understanding of who God is and start seeing *Him* as the most important person in her life?

That would settle her self-worth once and for all! To Jesus, she already is *somebody*. Like the loving father of the prodigal son, Jesus is frantically scanning the horizon, watching for Madonna to return to Him. He is absolutely convinced that she's so valuable that she's worth dying for. "Greater love has no one than this," said Jesus in John 15:13, "that one lay down his life for his friends." That's what He did for her on the cross!

Can you see how, over time, focusing on Jesus as the most important person in her life would get her off the treadmill of trying to draw her self-esteem from her fans?

I think Jesus would tell her, "I understand what happens when I'm missing from the core of a person's life. I understand how you feel compelled to search elsewhere for significance, affirmation, acceptance, self-worth, fulfillment, and love. That search has taken you to some dangerous and destructive places—and you still haven't found what you're looking for. You see, the frustration you feel is because the only thing that can really satisfy the center of your soul is *Me*."

Can you see that in your own life? Do you find yourself trying to measure your personal value by what your boss or parents or colleagues think of you? Are you keeping score by the number of promotions at work, the size of your investment portfolio, or the number of sexual encounters?

That struggle for self-worth, as Madonna conceded, will never end. As long as your value as a person is defined by another human being, you'll constantly be striving to prove to him or her that you're worthwhile. Only Jesus can pull the plug on that cycle. When you make Him the most important person in your life, then you *know* once and for all where you stand with Him.

He's firmly, irrevocably, unambiguously convinced that you're *somebody* worth dying for.

The Divine Adoption Process

So what should Madonna do? I think the answer is in the third pair of unexpected words from Jesus: "I'll help."

Even to someone as notorious as Madonna, I think Jesus would say, "I'll help you experience the fulfillment that has eluded you despite your struggle to find it. I'll help heal whatever's driving you to affirm your self-worth in self-defeating ways. *But I can only help you if you let Me*."

The Bible uses the metaphor of adoption. In Galatians 4 it says that God sent His Son so that we might be adopted as His children. This imagery seems especially appropriate for Madonna, whose loss of her mother at a young age helped fuel her lifelong search for affirmation.

One of Madonna's college friends said, "I felt like she just needed somebody to accept her, no questions asked." She was, in effect, a motherless child looking to be adopted by someone who would give her the no-strings-attached love that she longed for.

That reminds me of those heart-rending classified advertisements that some Sunday newspapers print under the heading, "Adoption." Through these ads desperate couples try to contact unwed pregnant women who might be willing to give up their child. The ads often bring tears to my eyes, like this one:

Imagine a childless couple providing your baby
with overflowing love, a wonderland of friends and family, the end of the rainbow, and the best that he or she
could be. We're a warmhearted, caring couple, ready to
share our lives, our hearts, and our home. Your baby will
have a lifetime of security, stability, and happiness with a
devoted mom and an adoring dad.

Think how vulnerable that couple was being by placing a
newspaper ad to tell the world how they're aching to pour out
their love on a child. And then think about how vulnerable God
allows Himself to be in the Bible. Basically, He's saying the same
thing. Actually, if God were to place one of those adoption ads, His
might say something like this:

I'll take the person who feels inadequate and
mediocre. I'll take the notorious and unworthy. I'll take
the person whose misguided quest for fulfillment has gotten her mired in immorality. I'll take the person who's
struggling with unanswered questions. I'll take the person
who's on the treadmill of trying to prove she's *somebody*.

And I'll provide a depth of love that she can't find
in empty sexuality. I'll provide the kind of fulfillment that
materialism will never buy. I'll offer satisfaction that will
endure even when the accolades stop. I'll provide the
security of a relationship that will continue into eternity.
And I'll give her brothers and sisters who will love her for
who she is—no questions asked.

Those are the arms that Madonna has been desperately
seeking! Who wouldn't want to be adopted by a loving Father like
that?

Instead of a phone number at the end of the ad, there might
be a verse taken right out of the pages of the apostle John's biography of Jesus. John 1:12 defines the divine adoption process very
clearly: "Yet to all who *received* him, to those who *believed* in his
name, he gave the right to *become* children of God."

When you extract the verbs I've highlighted, you've got a
precise equation for what it means to be welcomed into God's
family. It's *believe* + *receive* = *become*.

To *believe* means to have faith that Jesus is God, that He
died on the cross for our sins and was resurrected, and that He

offers eternal life as a free gift that cannot be earned. To *receive* means that we admit and turn away from our sin, embrace Jesus as our personal forgiver, and accept His gift of eternal life, which is a loving relationship with Him that begins immediately and continues forever. That's how we *become* one of His children.

That formula is a mind-boggling expression of the compassion and love that God is aching to pour out on each of us—if we'll let Him.

What kind of God is this, who prefers the human reclamation business to the human condemnation business? Like I said, when you get an accurate picture of who He is, He's awfully hard to resist.

Even for a Material Girl.

2

What Jesus Would Say to
Bart Simpson

A father from our church sat down with his family for dinner one night, and he asked his young son if he would say grace. After everyone folded their hands and bowed their heads, the youngster prayed, "Dear God, why should we thank You? *We* paid for this!"

The father was shocked. "Where in the world did you learn *that*?" he sputtered.

"From Bart Simpson," came the reply.

"Can you believe it?" the father said as he related the story to me. "He doesn't even watch the show; he picked that up from a commercial!"

Ah, yes, Bart Simpson, the imaginary ten-year-old, spike-haired, goggle-eyed fourth grader whom so many people love to hate. His national television program and product endorsements have established him as a cultural icon. One poll showed that more people know his name than the name of their own member of Congress. In fact, one person said, "I thought Bart Simpson *was* my congressman!"

Bart has been criticized from the White House to the schoolhouse, where some principals have banned his T-shirts that say, "Underachiever and proud of it!" That, of course, only fueled his popularity.

The Satirical Simpsons

So who is this dinky dude with an attitude? He's a wise-cracking video game addict who plays practical jokes, is disrespectful toward authority, uses profanity, and gets held after school to write repentant phrases on the blackboard, such as "I will not call my teacher 'hot cakes.'"

His bumbling dad, Homer, is a safety inspector at a nuclear power plant. Homer's parental advice includes such maxims as "Never say anything unless you're sure everyone feels exactly the same way." Bart's squeaky-voiced mother, Marge, is best known for her towering blue beehive hairdo. His sister, Lisa, is an eight-year-old saxophone virtuoso, while infant Maggie is perpetually plugged with a pacifier.

In other words, this is not the Huxtables. What it is, though, is satire—an exaggerated look at life from a kid's perspective, with a kernel of truth at its core.

For instance, because he's so uninhibited, Bart says things that other people only think. When he prays, "Why should we thank you, God—we bought this ourselves," people recoil in horror.

Yet isn't he just expressing a sentiment that a lot of people secretly harbor? They'd never *say* it, but don't many people live their lives with the attitude that they've earned what they've received and that God really had nothing to do with it? So, in some ways, Bart is merely more honest than most.

Spiritual matters are a recurring theme on the Simpson program. On one show Marge insisted that her youngsters visit church so they could "get a little goodness into them." Incidentally, this kind of desire to inculcate morals into children was a major reason why many Baby Boomers started returning to church in the early 1990s.

In Sunday school one child asked the teacher, "Will my dog, Fluffy, go to heaven?"

Caught off guard, the teacher didn't quite know how to respond. "Uh, no," she said, and the children looked disappointed.

Another asked, "How about my cat?"

"Uh, no," said the teacher. "Heaven is only for people."

But Bart pressed the issue. "Well, what if my leg gets gangrene and has to be amputated? Will it be waiting for me in heaven? And what about a robot with a human brain?"

"I don't know!" exclaimed the exasperated teacher. "Is a little blind faith too much to ask for?"

The show's creator, Matt Groening, also likes to poke fun at the chronically cheerful fundamentalist Christians who live next door to the Simpsons.

Jesus and Bart the Brat

But what would happen if Jesus Himself encountered little Bart, a child so annoying that his very name was derived from rearranging the letters in the word "brat"? What would Jesus do?

Would He heal Bart's hair? Would He give him a lesson on honoring his father and mother? Would He lecture him on honesty and tell him to stop stealing his sister's Monopoly money when she's not looking? Would He punish him for instigating food fights in the cafeteria? Or would he talk about Bart's self-proclaimed status as an underachiever? Maybe He'd encourage Bart by saying, "You know, through the years I've accomplished some of my best work through people who thought they didn't amount to much."

Jesus might talk about any of those topics. But based on His track record with children, I believe that if Jesus were to meet a real-life Bart Simpson, He wouldn't put him *over* His knee—instead, He'd put him *on* his knee. I think He'd talk to him in a loving and compassionate way. In fact, I could imagine Jesus saying, "Bart, I caught you doing something *right*."

You might ask, What could Bart Simpson have done right? Well, in one particularly poignant episode, Bart actually prayed a very heartfelt, sincere prayer. And I think Jesus might say, "Bart, you were headed down the correct road that night. Let's talk about prayer, because I'd like to reinforce what you did and help you go the next step in talking with God."

I know it sounds outrageous that we might learn about prayer from Bart Simpson, but it's not unprecedented. Other cartoon characters have taught us some things about prayer in the past.

For instance, remember Linus, the kid with the blanket in the *Peanuts* cartoon? One day while he was talking to Lucy with his hands folded, he said, "I think I've made a new theological discovery. If you hold your hands upside down, you get the opposite of what you pray for!"

Okay, so that's not very helpful. But I do believe we *can* learn some basics about prayer from Bart's experience in talking to God about a crisis he encountered at school.

The Day Bart Prayed

Bart wasn't doing very well in the fourth grade. When he flunked his book report on *Treasure Island* because he knew only what was on the cover, that was the last straw. His teacher called a meeting with Bart's parents and the school psychologist, whose conclusion was that Bart should repeat the fourth grade.

Bart was horrified! "Look at my eyes," he said. "See the sincerity? See the conviction? See the fear? I swear I'll do better!" After all, nothing's worse to a ten-year-old than being held back in school.

Then Bart hatched a plan. He made a deal with a brainy student named Martin. He'd teach Martin how to be cool if Martin would help him pass his next American history exam. That final test was monumentally important because if he passed it, Bart would be allowed to graduate.

Bart did teach Martin the fine points of being cool—how to burp on command, spray-paint graffiti on garage doors, and shoot a slingshot at unsuspecting girls. And, sure enough, Martin became the most popular student in school—so popular, in fact, that he didn't have time to help Bart study!

Now picture this: It was the night before the big test. Bart was sitting at the desk in his room, staring at an open book, trying to study, when he came to the chilling realization that it was too late. He couldn't cram enough into his head in one night to be able to pass the test. Finally, his mom peeked into the room and said, "It's past your bedtime, Bart."

Slowly, Bart closed his book. With the exam just hours away, it seemed like all his options had evaporated. That's when he got down on his knees next to his bed and prayed to God.

"This is hopeless!" he said. "Well, Old Timer, I guess this is the end of the road. I know I haven't been a good kid, but if I have to go to school tomorrow, I'll fail the test and be held back. I just need one more day to study, Lord. I need Your help! A teacher strike, a power failure, a blizzard—anything that will cancel school tomorrow. I know it's asking a lot, but if anyone can do it, You can. Thanking You in advance, your pal, Bart Simpson."

The scene switched to an outside view of Bart's house. The lights in his room went out. It was cold and dark. A few moments passed, and then a single snowflake gently fell to the ground. Then another. And another. Suddenly there was a virtual avalanche of snow; in fact, it was the biggest blizzard in the city's history! The *Hallelujah Chorus* swelled in the background.

The next day school was canceled. Bart fought the temptation to go sledding with his friends and instead studied hard. Then the following day, when the time finally came for the test, he gave it his best shot. Even so, he came up one point short. It looked like he had failed—until, at the last possible moment, he miraculously scored one extra-credit point and squeaked by with a D-minus.

Bart was so happy that he kissed his teacher as he scampered out the door. Homer was so overwhelmed that he posted Bart's paper on the refrigerator and declared, "I'm proud of you, boy."

To which Bart replied: "Thanks, Dad. But part of this D-minus belongs to God."

What Bart Did Right

Isn't that great? If Bart were a *real* boy and he prayed a *real* prayer like that, I think Jesus would say, "Bart, there are four major things you did right. Let's talk about them. The first thing you did right was this: You prayed directly from your heart."

One recent survey showed that while talking to God is a nearly universal activity among Americans, more than one-third of them merely recite formula prayers when they communicate with Him.

But Bart didn't just repeat some fancy language he had learned in Sunday school. He didn't try to lower his voice two octaves. He talked to God directly from his heart, pouring out his frustrations and fears.

Why did he feel so free to do that? One reason is that he was alone with God at the time. The Bible says in Matthew 6:6, "When you pray, go into your room, close the door and pray to your Father, who is unseen. Then your Father, who sees what is done in secret, will reward you."

That makes sense, doesn't it? If I have something very intimate I want to say to my wife, Leslie, I don't want to say it in front of others, even if they're friends. I wait until Leslie and I are alone.

Now, there's nothing wrong with group prayer, public prayer, or praying with your spouse. Those can be quite appropriate and beneficial. But there's no substitute for regular, one-on-one, heart-to-heart talks between just you and God—when you're not trying to impress anybody else with your spirituality, put a positive spin on a bad situation, or hold anything back.

Are you creating those opportunities for yourself? For Christians who are deeply involved in church, it's easy to feel that the praying they do in ministry settings is enough. But it's not. We all need to get alone with God—whether it's in the morning, during lunch, or at night—so we can feel the uninhibited freedom to be vulnerable and honest with Him.

If necessary, do what I've done on occasion: In the midst of busy periods, when I'm most susceptible to forgetting to connect with God, I make an "appointment" with Him in my daily schedule. I actually write in, "12:30: Meet with God." That way I make sure I've set aside some time for a heart-to-heart talk.

"This Is Hopeless!"

Another reason Bart was so willing to sincerely call out for help can be found in the first three words he spoke: "This is hopeless!"

Bart's back was against the wall. He had tried to extricate himself from the jam he was in, but he couldn't. And so, all of a sudden, where's the smart-aleck Bart? The profane Bart? The Bart who tweaks authority? The Bart who prays irreverent prayers?

They've disappeared. Bart has come face-to-face with the fact that he's helpless, and when any of us comes to that realization, that's when our self-sufficiency vanishes, our cockiness disappears, and our wise-guy attitude melts into sincerity. That's when we pray directly from the heart.

"Nothing so furthers our prayer life as the feeling of our own helplessness," Ole Hallesby wrote in his classic book *Prayer*. "It is only when we are helpless that we really open our hearts to God."

I'm convinced that one way we can keep our prayers alive and coming from our heart is to keep our helplessness at the very forefront of our minds. A daily acknowledgment of our dependence on God dramatically heightens our desperation for His intervention in our lives.

And let's face it—despite the image of competence that we like to project, we *are* helpless in the things that really matter. At least, I know I am. For instance:

• Jesus tells me to forgive my enemies and to return good for evil. But I have trouble forgiving the guy who holds me up for a few minutes by driving ten miles an hour under the speed limit, much less someone who has actually hurt or insulted me.

• Jesus says, "Be anxious for nothing," but on my own I tend to fall victim to worry. By myself, I'm helpless to live in confidence and peace.

• Jesus calls on me to live a holy life, but I feel tempted all the time to take another path, and I'm helpless to resist that day after day on my own.

• Jesus says to be outrageously generous to the poor, but my human tendency is to want to cling to my possessions. Left to myself, I tend to draw my security from my things rather than from my God.

• Jesus tells me to be sacrificial in my love for others, but my inclination is to put my own needs first. In and of myself, I'm incapable of consistently living out that kind of life.

In fact, Jesus said in John 15:5, "Apart from Me you can do nothing." And I've found that when I keep that truth in mind day by day and express my helplessness to God up front, *that's* when my prayers really come from my heart. *It's when I shed the pretense of self-sufficiency that I become desperate for the sufficiency of Christ.*

Hallesby calls this "the blessed attitude of helplessness before God." Is that your approach to prayer? If not, try taking a few moments to honestly appraise your own helplessness before you address God.

When you remind yourself that you're fundamentally incapable of living a God-honoring lifestyle under your own power, then you reach out all the more fervently for God's help and guidance. And you walk away from your time in prayer with renewed confidence in Philippians 4:13, which says: "I can do everything through him who gives me strength."

I think Jesus would say to Bart, "I'm glad you didn't feel compelled to pray a nice, neat, theologically perfect little ditty. You cried from your heart out of your own helplessness, and that moves the heart of God just as the cry of a helpless infant moves the heart of his loving parents. Bart, I liked the way you prayed."

From Father to Daddy

Second, I believe that Jesus would encourage Bart about the way in which he addressed God. Remember how Bart called God "Old Timer"? I think Jesus might say, "I know that was a term of trust and endearment from you, and that's a big step toward seeing God as being approachable in a crisis. But let Me clue you in on something: There's another approach to addressing God that can revolutionize the way you envision Him."

You see, one of the most radical and countercultural things Jesus did during His ministry was to call God "My Father." Every time He said it—and many instances are recorded—He was turning generations of Jewish tradition upside down.

In ancient Jewish writings, the term "Father" was applied to God only occasionally, and when it was, it was used in a very general sense, as in the Father of creation. For instance, Malachi 2:10 says, "Have we not all one Father? Did not one God create us?"

36

But you won't find a single instance in which there was such a personal reference to God as the term "My Father." In fact, British theologian Michael Green said, "You can search Islam, and you will not find that name of Father among the ninety-nine names of God. You will search Hinduism or Confucianism in vain. This is unique."

What's more, Jesus didn't merely call Him "Father." He used a word for Father that would be the modern equivalent of calling Him "Daddy" or "Papa." It's the term that a small child would use in talking intimately with a parent. Even when Jesus was in the Garden of Gethsemane, wrestling with the anguish of having to face the cross, He called out to the Father as "Daddy."

Of course, Jesus had a special relationship with the Father stretching back through eternity, and so you might expect that He would address Him in this intensely personal way. But then Jesus did something even more radical: He told His followers, "You can call Him 'Daddy,' too. I'm giving you permission."

Isn't that incredible? What an amazing privilege! I'll never forget what someone told me shortly after I became a Christian: "Lee, think of all the great spiritual giants of the Old Testament—Moses and Isaiah and Daniel and Abraham and David—and then remember that not one of them was ever given the privilege of addressing God as intimately as 'Daddy.' But as a follower of Jesus, He has given *you* that honor. Never take it lightly!"

One problem is that when we think of God as our Father, it's only natural for us to subconsciously ascribe to Him the attributes of our own natural father. And often, our earthly father has fallen far short of the ideal. Think of Bart—he's got Homer for a father, and clearly he's no Ward Cleaver or Dr. Huxtable. So what can we do when the image of our earthly father distorts our perception of our heavenly Father?

The answer can be found in John 14:9, where Jesus said, "Anyone who has seen me has seen the Father." In other words, delve into the life of Jesus. Study a biography of Him, such as the gospel of John or Luke. And through reading about His love, His patience, His power, and His desire to help people, He can create for you a more concrete picture of what your heavenly Father is like.

And then, if you're a follower of Jesus and want to take your communication with God to the next level of intimacy, try this: The next time you're alone with God, call Him "Daddy." *What I've found is that you can't talk to God as "Daddy" and at the same time feel that He's some distant, detached, or disinterested deity.*

I know it's awkward at first. At least, it was for me. It seems almost too personal, too presumptuous. But when I do it, it brings home to me that I really am God's child, and that He loves me with a tenderness and compassion that goes beyond the love of even my natural father.

And so the next time you need to feel that special reassurance, go ahead and call out to Him as your "Daddy."

Bart Comes Clean

After Jesus talked to Bart about the way he prayed and addressed God, I think He'd turn His attention to the third thing Bart did right, which was the way he referred to himself in his prayer.

When Bart said, "I know I haven't been a good kid," that was a monumental step for him to take. After all, whenever Bart is caught doing something wrong, his immediate response has always been: "I didn't do it—nobody saw me do it—you can't prove I did it!" Bart's like a bulletproof vest when it comes to deflecting blame. But in his prayer, he actually admitted that he had messed up. And I think Jesus would say, "Bart, that's a good beginning."

Confession is one of the most critically important—but often overlooked—aspects of prayer. In fact, if you feel like there's static in your prayer line to God, maybe it's because your unconfessed sin is interfering with the signal.

The wrongdoing we commit, even as followers of Jesus, strains our relationship with God if we leave it unresolved. It's sort of like what happened when you were a child and your mother knew you had done something wrong, but you didn't know she knew. When you pretended everything was perfectly all right, didn't that put tension in your relationship? All your mother wanted was for you to come clean with her—and that's exactly the step God wants us to take.

It's pretty easy to do it like Bart, who merely admitted that he had fallen short of being good. It's not very difficult for people to say, "I'm a sinner," especially when the Bible says we're *all* in that boat. What's humbling is when we're painfully specific—and yet that's where true liberation lies. "He who conceals his sins does not prosper," says Proverbs 28:13, "but whoever confesses and renounces them finds mercy."

I've learned a lot about prayer from my mentor, Bill Hybels, and one thing he has always emphasized is, "Don't gloss over your sin." More than once, he has reminded me that the only time a person is truly being honest with himself and forthright with God is when he gets explicit about his transgressions.

It's when I say to God, "Yesterday I misled my assistant into thinking I was doing one thing when I really was doing another." Or, "During that meeting yesterday, I puffed myself up and at the same time subtly deflated others." Or, "I've been holding a grudge against someone even though I know I should forgive him." Or, "I callously passed up several opportunities this week to help the poor." Or, "I gossiped about my supervisor behind his back."

That demonstrates to God that we're serious about dealing with our sin. And when we say, "I'm sorry for these transgressions, and I thank You for forgiving me totally and completely," that's a terrific way to clear our conscience.

It's a great deterrent, too. "When you're totally honest about your sins, something happens," Hybels wrote in his book *Too Busy Not to Pray*. "About the fifth day in a row that you have to call yourself a liar, a greedy person, a manipulator or whatever, you say to yourself, 'I'm tired of admitting that. With God's power, I've got to root it out of my life.'"

Are you taking the time to deal honestly with your sin before God? He already knows your foul-ups. He's just waiting for you to stop pretending and to 'fess up—for your own sake, and for the sake of your relationship with Him.

At least Bart took a step in that direction, although it's unclear whether he had an attitude of genuine repentance. And without pushing it *too* far, there are several other things he did right in his prayer that we can emulate:

- He humbly asked for the desire of his heart—that somehow he would get one more day to study. Philippians 4:6 says, "In everything, by prayer and petition, with thanksgiving, present your requests to God."

• Bart expressed at least a modicum of faith when he said, "I know it's asking a lot, but if anyone can do it, You can." Hebrews 11:6 says, "Without faith, it is impossible to please God."

• And he gave God credit for having helped him. Remember when he said part of his D-minus belonged to God?

"Your Pal, Bart Simpson"

But I think the last major observation of Jesus might be to look at the way Bart concluded his prayer, because it says a lot about the way he sees God. Bart signed his verbal letter to the Lord with, "Your pal, Bart Simpson." And I think Jesus might reply:

"Bart, I'm so glad you're starting to think of Me as your pal. Not only do I want you to receive Me as the forgiver of your sins and the leader of your life, but I also want to be your friend.

"And yet this goes further than you might realize. Think of what real pals do. Sure, a pal goes to his friend's rescue when he's in trouble. But pals hang around with each other in the good times, too. They confide in each other, care about each other, and are honest with each other. Pals talk to each other all the time. They get comfortable around each other. They love and serve each other. That, Bart, is what pals do."

Jesus told His followers in John 15:15: "I have called you friends." And that's what Jesus would want with any real-life Bart Simpson—a day-to-day friendship that would deepen through the years. A relationship that could transform even a brat like Bart into a fully devoted follower of Christ.

The key that opens this kind of relationship is in the hands of each of us. "I stand at the door and knock," Jesus said in Revelation 3:20. "If anyone hears my voice and opens the door, I will go in and eat with him, and he with me."

What a terrific picture of friendship: The God of the universe having a meal with someone like you or me. And what a mind-boggling thought: that we can talk with God just like we would talk with our closest friend over a quiet and intimate dinner.

Does that describe your relationship with God? If not, He's knocking—and the key to the door is in your hands.

Spitballs and Spirituality

Those are some of the comments Jesus might make to Bart. Admittedly Bart's prayer wasn't a perfect model; if you want the best illustration of how to pray, consult Matthew 6:9–13, where Jesus personally taught His followers how to talk with God. But don't you think that Bart did all right for a kid who's more famous for spitballs than spirituality?

And maybe—as outrageous as it sounds—we can come away with a few ideas about how to notch up our own interaction with God.

Because if we resolve to regularly spend quality time alone with God; if we approach prayer with an attitude of our own helplessness; if we think about God not as some detached deity but as our "Daddy," who loves us more than any earthly father can; if we consistently confess our wrongdoing so we unclog our lines of communication with God; and if we really begin to live out the implications of having God as our friend—then even a spike-haired little terror like Bart Simpson will have done a good deed for the day.

To which an aghast Bart would probably exclaim, "Aye, karumba!"

3

What Jesus Would Say to
Rush Limbaugh

Greetings, conversationalists across the fruited plain, this is Rush Limbaugh, the most dangerous man in America, serving humanity simply by opening my mouth, destined for my own wing in the Museum of Broadcasting, executing everything I do flawlessly with zero mistakes, doing this show with half my brain tied behind my back just to make it fair, because I have talent on loan from God. Rush Limbaugh. A man. A legend. A way of life.

So begins another radio broadcast of the country's most controversial—and unlikely—political commentator. The product of a small Missouri river town, a college dropout who flunked Speech 101 and was fired from a half dozen radio jobs, a twice-divorced proclaimer of family values, a promoter of patriotism who didn't register to vote until he was thirty-five, Limbaugh has become a force so powerful that some industry insiders have credited him with single-handedly resuscitating AM radio.

In fact, this staunchly conservative pundit has blossomed into a one-man conglomerate. He has gone from being broke twice in recent years to earning an estimated $20 million in 1993.

By 1994 his three-hour daily radio program was airing on more than 625 stations with twenty million listeners. His nightly national TV show rakes in $24,000 for thirty seconds of commercial time. His monthly newsletter boasts 370,000 subscribers. He pockets $30,000 for his "Rush to Excellence" road shows, which he has performed up to forty times a year. He sells tens of thousands of videos at $24.95 apiece. His first book, *The Way Things Ought to Be*, sold more than three million copies, and his second book, *See, I Told You So*, had the biggest first printing in American history. And that doesn't count the Rush coffee mugs and T-shirts!

His product is simple: It's Rush Hudson Limbaugh III, *sans* script, sitting alone at a microphone or staring into a camera, enthusiastically and often humorously prescribing a conservative cure for what's ailing America.

And who is Rush Limbaugh? That, of course, depends on who you ask. As for himself, Limbaugh claims to be "just a harmless little fuzz ball."

But talk show host Larry King judges him guilty of "gay-bashing, bashing women, bashing blacks." Humorist Erma Bombeck has called him "Rush Slimebaugh." ABC's Jeff Greenfield thinks he's "very funny." Brian Keliher, who publishes the *Flush Rush Quarterly*, fears that he's a "godlike creature" to his fans. *Vanity Fair* called him the "patron saint of white male chauvinists." Says *Nightline's* Ted Koppel: "He's very smart. He does his homework."

To *Newsweek*, he's "the American White Male under siege, coping with femi-Nazis, dolphin huggers, 'wacko' environmentalists and closet 'socialists' such as Bill Clinton." *Playboy* painted him as being "William F. Buckley without the thesaurus; Pat Buchanan without the mean-spiritedness; Ross Perot without the paranoia." Ronald Reagan gave him the ultimate Republican salute by calling him "the number one voice for conservatism in our country."

So who is he, *really*? What is he saying that has so many people listening? And what, in the end, might Jesus have to say to him?

Will the Real Rush Please Stand Up?

Time magazine featured a revealing anecdote in a 1993 cover story about Limbaugh. It said that at a symposium for the media elite on the East Coast, the audience burst into applause after ABC's Sam Donaldson condemned Limbaugh for calling some feminists femi-Nazis and for "his *ad hominem* attacks and ghoulish humor." But when the clapping died down, Republican strategist Mary Matalin asked how many had ever actually listened to Limbaugh.

"Silence," she recalled. "Absolute silence. Nothing. Nobody."

The Bible has been called the most criticized but least read book in the world. And similarly, in talking to people about Limbaugh, I've found that some of his most vociferous critics are those who have never or rarely listened to him.

For instance, when columnist William Raspberry, who is an African-American, found out Limbaugh had agreed with him on a couple of issues, he implied Limbaugh was a racist and said, "I don't need bouquets from a guy like this."

That brought so many protests that Raspberry later wrote: "I confess now that, apart from a couple of accidental listenings, I didn't know that much about Limbaugh. I still don't. My opinions about him had come largely from other people—mostly friends who think Rush is a four-letter word. They are certain he is a bigot. But is he?"

Raspberry admitted he couldn't find any racist remarks by the broadcaster. "Limbaugh is often [for many of us] the hated opinion, but that doesn't, by itself, make him hateful," Raspberry concluded.

"I'm not a bigot. I am not a racist, a homophobe, male chauvinist pig, or any of that," Limbaugh has insisted. "What I am . . . is antiliberal. Liberalism is a scourge. It destroys the human spirit. It destroys prosperity. It assigns sameness to everybody. And wherever I find it, I oppose it."

Usually that means combating it with a potent arsenal of satire and offbeat humor, a clever tactic since studies have shown that people are more receptive to new ideas when they're laughing. Even quite a few liberals admit they tune in to be entertained.

"It's the oddest thing," wrote *Detroit Free Press* columnist Bob Talbert. "I hate many of Rush Limbaugh's antiquated and archaic attitudes, yet I love his show." One study showed that nearly three times as many people listen to Limbaugh for entertainment rather than because he represents their viewpoint.

"Imagine that—a funny conservative," Limbaugh quipped. "Isn't that a novelty? What a great circus America has become!"

As the clown prince of conservatism, Limbaugh relentlessly lampoons the political left and chides the liberal media. He once said that if the planet were approaching its last day, the *Washington Post's* headline would read: "World Ends Tomorrow—Women, Minorities Hardest Hit!"

He skewers animal rights extremists with his "Animal Updates," which are introduced by Andy Williams's song "Born Free" being played over background sounds of shotgun blasts, mortar fire, and squealing animals. His approach, Limbaugh says, is to illustrate absurdity by being absurd.

However, Limbaugh's repeated claim that he's "just an entertainer" drastically understates his increasingly influential role in the country's political and social debate. If he were merely into entertainment, he wouldn't have been asked to discuss politics on journalist David Brinkley's program or weighty military issues on *Nightline*. After all, you don't see Cher being invited to discuss national security with Ted Koppel.

And he wouldn't be holding weekend forums for big-name conservatives to promote their ideology. Nor would he have been greeted as a hero at the 1992 Republican convention, where the Astrodome crowd chanted "Rush, Rush!" as he sat next to the vice president's wife. When Limbaugh wowed the packed crowd at a $75-a-person gathering during the convention, Paul Colford, author of *The Rush Limbaugh Story*, observed, "Only Ronald Reagan would have whipped up lustier cheers."

More recently Limbaugh seems willing to admit his impact on the political scene. In one interview he claimed that by 1996 he will be able, if he chooses, to control *twenty million* votes in the presidential race—a bloc that clearly has the potential of swinging the nomination.

Who *is* Rush Limbaugh? His supporters and detractors agree: He's someone not to be ignored.

The Rushian Gospel

Limbaugh traces his conservative outlook to his late father, a successful lawyer who "told you what he believed full brunt force, right between the eyes." His dad would spend hours regaling young Rush and his friends with his colorful commentary on politics and ethics. And his father, who taught Sunday school and directed the choir at a United Methodist Church, also gave Limbaugh the religious training that has helped shape his outlook.

"It [religion] caused us to believe in family values," Limbaugh's brother, David, told Michael Arkush for the biography, *Rush!* "My dad used to say morality descends from God, that human beings wouldn't have a moral code if it didn't come from God, and we'd live in a state of anarchy. We don't believe in moral relativism, secular humanism; we believe in God and immutable laws, the primacy of the human species. From that flow a lot of his political views."

Limbaugh's popularity among fundamentalist and evangelical Christians—by one estimate, twenty to twenty-five percent of his audience—stems in part from the way he uses biblical themes to advance his brand of conservatism. He refers to God on a regular basis and even quotes the Bible from time to time.

"There is not a day that goes by that I do not think about the existence of God and what it means and where we came from," Limbaugh told *The Door* in an interview. He said that he has a personal faith in Christ, adding: "Jesus holds the answers to all of the everyday problems that you face. I'm talking about an acceptance and belief in Jesus, heaven, and God."

Many of his views are firmly rooted in Scripture. For instance, he believes that because God created human life, it's sacred and therefore abortion and euthanasia are wrong; that because people were made in God's image, they're fundamentally different and more valuable than animals—that God gave people dominion over the planet. Limbaugh believes that God established the family, and therefore it needs to be kept strong by society; that God's laws concerning sexuality and morality are unchanging and still applicable today; and that everybody should be held personally responsible for their actions. He believes that the country's Judeo-Christian heritage should be nurtured, and that the First

Amendment wasn't intended to protect people *from* religion but to protect religious people from government interference.

As far as all of this goes, how could any Bible-believing Christian disagree? Jesus would certainly applaud these particular values as being consistent with the teachings of Scripture, wouldn't He?

But Dr. Daniel J. Evearitt, a specialist in religion and popular culture at Toccoa Falls College in Georgia, raises some cautions about Limbaugh's overall approach. "The 'gospel' that Rush Limbaugh preaches," he said, "is heavy on the societal implications of religion and light on a theology of personal redemption."

In other words Limbaugh stresses the benefits to society of following God's moral standards, and while those benefits are great, the only way America will ever *really* be transformed is when individuals, one by one, open themselves to the life-changing power of Jesus Christ.

"He appears to be vastly more interested in renewing and redeeming society than in personal salvation," wrote Evearitt in his book *Rush Limbaugh and the Bible*. "Important as our religious roots and belief in God are, standing alone they are insufficient to remedy man's malady. The fundamental issue of human sin must be dealt with on an individual basis by repentance for sin and acceptance of salvation through Jesus Christ."

It's that ugly tendency toward personal sin—selfishness, indifference, self-indulgence, animosity toward others—that's actually at the root of the social issues that Limbaugh seeks to address through political means. Jesus' agenda is to relentlessly but lovingly focus on our sin problem because that's the sticking point that keeps us from enjoying community with Him and each other.

Christ's emphasis, then, is on a *spiritual* kingdom at this point, not a political one, so He probably wouldn't engage Limbaugh in a debate over the intricacies of NATO or NAFTA. After all, well-meaning Christians can disagree over how biblical values get translated into specific governmental policies, which is why it's dangerous and misleading for any political persuasion to claim Christ's exclusive endorsement.

But there would still be plenty for Jesus to talk over with Limbaugh—and, as we know, Limbaugh is seldom without words himself.

Jesus Talks with Rush

Rush Limbaugh has dined with world leaders, slept in the White House, and hobnobbed with celebrities. But an eyeball-to-eyeball rendezvous with Jesus Christ—well, *that* would certainly be a fascinating encounter!

Jesus would probably establish pretty quickly that He's not just another "dittohead," which is Limbaugh's term for those whose views are in such absolute sync with his that they automatically say "ditto" to his every pronouncement. Even so, I think Jesus would be, in characteristic fashion, both affirming as well as challenging.

"Rush," I could imagine Him saying, "a lot of your values are like a page right out of My own book, and I'm very pleased by that. In a day when America's airwaves feature more filth than faith, it's refreshing when My name receives respect instead of rebuke. So, Rush, let Me encourage you—whenever you look to Me and My teachings for guidance, you're looking in the right direction."

But then I think there are two areas Jesus would want to discuss with Limbaugh—*what* he's communicating as well as *how* he's communicating. You see, *both* are important to God. "If I speak in the tongues of men and of angels, but have not love, I am only a resounding gong or a clanging cymbal," wrote the apostle Paul in 1 Corinthians 13:1.

To Jesus, unless we're motivated by love—the kind of love a Christ-revolutionized heart, over time, expresses more and more—then whatever we say or do lacks real merit or meaning. Now *that's* challenging, isn't it?

Jesus might say, "Rush, let's talk for a few moments about the way in which you speak to your listeners—both your attitude and your approach. The Bible can provide you with some guidance in Ephesians 4:15, where it basically says this: Speak the truth, but do it in love."

The Wedding of Truth and Love

There are many great truths of God that America desperately needs to hear and to respond to. But the way in which they're communicated can either challenge and motivate or alienate and divide. Unfortunately Limbaugh's style has often ended up unnecessarily driving wedges between people.

Although Limbaugh claims to be presenting the truth about America—"The views expressed on this show have been documented to be correct 97.7 percent of the time"—Limbaugh actually takes a caricature approach to politics.

He essentially paints "liberals" as always having bad motives and never being right and "conservatives" as always having good motives and never being wrong. He gives every benefit of the doubt to conservatives while reading sinister intentions into virtually every position others take. For instance, he criticizes Vice President Al Gore for flip-flopping on abortion, while he naively accepts former President George Bush's claim that politics played no role in his own reversal on the issue. And Limbaugh often wildly exaggerates his opponents' positions—such as when he said that if the Democrats were in power during the first century, they would probably "demand" that Mary have an abortion because Jesus was "an unwanted pregnancy."

The result of Limbaugh's approach is the creation of a simplistic and unrealistic "good guys versus bad guys" mentality that short-circuits meaningful discussion and precludes constructive compromises.

He also polarizes people along gender lines. While denying he's sexist, Limbaugh repeatedly makes degrading, off-color remarks about women. He says he likes the women's movement—"especially when viewed from behind." He has referred to two feminists as "a couple of ugly dogs" and said the feminist movement is led by women who "can't get a man, and their rage is one long PMS attack." At one point he even refused to accept phone calls from women unless they first sent him their photo.

His use of volatile terms like "femi-Nazis" merely inflames emotions and pushes people away. I've met Limbaugh supporters who use that word like a weapon to wound any woman who asserts her legitimate rights. Limbaugh insists the term applies only to the most radical, man-hating feminists, such as those "to whom the most important thing in life is seeing to it that every abortion possible happens." But how many American women are like that? Limbaugh admits there are only twenty or so, yet his frequent use of the term has spurred some of his followers to wield it indiscriminately.

In fact, any regular Limbaugh listener knows that he panders to our tendency to name-call and categorize people. Instead of staying on a responsible track in discussing homosexuality, for example, Colford said Limbaugh has used the derogatory term "faggot" on his program.

In his book *The Way Things Ought to Be*, Limbaugh wrote: "Real problems deserve real solutions, not name-calling." Now that sounds like a positive position—except that it's defeated four sentences later when he calls advocates for the poor "poverty pimps."

The sad truth is that it's much easier for all of us to dismiss and trivialize others after we label and then relegate them to an undesirable category. At least, I've found that's true in my life. I'm much more apt to disregard or devalue people after I mentally put them into the "troublemaker" or "unimportant" or "different" classification. Once I've done that, it's a small step to say I have no moral responsibility toward them.

The cure, I've learned, is to keep reminding myself over and over that each person—regardless of his or her politics, philosophy, or personality—has intrinsic worth as an image-bearer of God. Simply put, they matter to Him, so they should matter to me.

Overall, there's no question that Limbaugh raises some important topics. But they cry out for a balanced Christian perspective—and that means truthfully addressing the issues without denigrating others through vulgarities, stereotypes, or unfair and simplistic characterizations.

"That," Jesus might say to Limbaugh, "is part of what it means to speak the truth in love."

Bastion of Noncompassion?

Another test of whether we're speaking the truth in love is how and what we communicate about the disenfranchised members of society. Jesus was a friend to the poor and the sick, caring about them and treating them with dignity and respect. And He might say to Limbaugh, "As I've poured out My compassion on you, I want you to express it to those who are in need. As Proverbs 14:31 says, 'Whoever is kind to the needy honors God.'"

The poor are a frequent subject of Limbaugh's commentaries. He has criticized liberals for loudly declaring compassion toward the homeless and other people in need, but then prescribing misguided governmental remedies that merely worsen the problem. In the end, he says, that kind of empty sympathy doesn't really benefit anybody.

Limbaugh's approach would be to help the poor overcome their dependence on the government and work toward self-reliance wherever possible—laudable goals which, if achieved, would certainly improve their lifestyle. "You people should understand that I am not some bastion of noncompassion, without any concern for my fellow man," Limbaugh wrote in *The Way Things Ought to Be*.

While much of his critique of the homeless situation and proposals for helping the poor make sense, some of Limbaugh's remarks have called his attitude into question. He seems to view the problems of the poor as a societal issue, divorced from the reality that these are real people who are hurting and who need compassion and love as much as they need political proposals for improving their lot.

For instance, according to the *Los Angeles Times*, he told a wildly applauding audience: "One of the things I want to do before I die is conduct the Homeless Olympics." Among the events would be "the ten-meter Shopping Cart Relay, the Dumpster Dig, and the Hop, Skip, and Trip." Stop for a moment and think about what kind of message that sends his dittoheads about the attitude they should express toward the needy.

Limbaugh raised legitimate questions about the activities of homeless advocate Mitch Snyder, but he couldn't resist ridiculing him even after Snyder committed suicide. To a laughing audience, Limbaugh referred to the deceased Snyder as having "assumed room temperature" and said he had "finally earned a home." He also conducted a tongue-in-cheek "requiem mass" for him and even jokingly speculated whether he had been mentioned in his suicide note.

In addition, biographer Arkush says Limbaugh once held a contest "to see which of the cities that carried his show would charter the first bus of 'indigents and illegal aliens' to the 'left coast.'" His idea was to poke fun at actor Martin Sheen's declaration of Malibu, California, as a sanctuary for the poor. But as Arkush said, "Once again, Rush was perceived as insensitive to a very serious problem in America."

To Jesus our attitude toward the needy really matters. In fact, He might remind Limbaugh of this chilling warning found in Proverbs 17:5: "He who mocks the poor shows contempt for their Maker."

In other words God is insulted when anyone belittles His handiwork—and the poor are etched with His likeness every bit as much as the wealthy. Christ demonstrated compassion for the disenfranchised members of society through both word *and* deed, through both truth *and* love. That's the pattern He challenges His people to follow.

Jesus also said that the way we treat the sick in society is the way we're treating Him. "Whatever you did for one of the least of these brothers of mine, you did for me" (Matt. 25:40).

And yet during a two-week period, Limbaugh featured an "AIDS Update," using Dionne Warwick's song, "I'll Never Love This Way Again" as one of the theme songs. By Limbaugh's own admission, these updates "ended up making fun of people who were dying long, painful, and excruciating deaths."

To his credit he later apologized, saying that "it was a totally irresponsible thing to do." But in the meantime his parodies fueled the prejudice suffered by many AIDS patients.

Now, nobody can claim a perfect record of being a consistent ambassador of Christ's compassion. As for me, I'm glad the times that I've been insensitive—and, I regret to say, there have been many—haven't been broadcast to twenty million listeners.

But that's the point: Limbaugh sets the tone for multitudes of listeners. He has a rare platform to propose meaningful societal reforms for helping the needy and at the same time inspire his listeners to take personal and sacrificial steps to serve them in love.

It's too easy—and too offensive to God—to merely debate them as a political topic.

On an individual level, the real issue is how we respond when we realize we've been cold-blooded in our approach and attitude. Do we offer a surface-level apology without changing our conduct, risking the buildup of calluses on our hearts? Or do we seek Christ's forgiveness and ask Him to help us see His face when we look at the needy?

"Rush, you've been courageous several times by admitting that you've been insensitive," Jesus might say. "That shows character, and I want you to know that My forgiveness is always available to you. And what's more, I'll be there to help you communicate compassionately about the homeless and the sick. When you think about them, consider this: I loved them enough to die for them."

Says Proverbs 31:8–9: "Speak up for those who cannot speak for themselves, for the rights of all who are destitute. Speak up and judge fairly; defend the rights of the poor and needy."

Taking Aim at Amy

As the credits rolled across the screen at the end of one of Limbaugh's TV programs, alert viewers spotted the name of a new head writer: Bill Clinton.

It was a joke, of course, but also an acknowledgment that Clinton's administration has provided a mother lode of material for Limbaugh. Some predicted Limbaugh's popularity would fizzle once Clinton took office; instead it has sizzled.

Certainly there's nothing wrong in a democracy with critiquing and even satirizing the powers that be. But while almost anything goes under the First Amendment, I think Jesus would remind Limbaugh that, spiritually speaking, there's a line of disrespect that His followers shouldn't cross.

Truth—even hard truth, compellingly presented and passionately defended—needs to be tempered by love and respect.

"This is also why you pay taxes, for the authorities are God's servants, who give their full time to governing," the apostle Paul wrote in Romans 13:6–7. "Give everyone what you owe him:

If you owe taxes, pay taxes; if revenue, then revenue; if *respect*, then *respect*; if *honor*, then *honor*."

In addition, 1 Timothy 2:1–2 calls on Christians to pray for "all those in authority," while Titus 3 forbids the slandering of those in government.

The problem is that Limbaugh poisons the pond of public debate when he slips from legitimate discussion of public issues to personal attacks by making fun of the appearance, speech, and even the physical size of his political foes.

For instance, instead of sticking to an analysis of Jimmy Carter's actions as president, he stooped to declaring that Carter's daughter, Amy, was the ugliest presidential daughter ever. (That cruel remark brought a wet-noodle reprimand from Limbaugh's mother, who said: "People can't help the way they look. And, besides, you forgot Margaret Truman Daniel.")

He referred to Alan Cranston as "former U.S. cadaver— ahem, senator," and to Jim Wright as "the former Sleazer of the House." He has often chided one of Clinton's cabinet members for being short. On his TV show, while showing a videotape of a government official giving a speech, he frequently mocks their mannerisms, personal style, or the way they pronounce certain words. While he can be funny, the humor comes at a cost.

"As a conservative he advocates respect for authority," said Evearitt, "but when he ridicules elected officials he undercuts that very authority."

What's more, he undercuts his credibility as a Christian when he encourages his viewers to reduce political debate to below-the-belt blows. "Remind the people to be subject to rulers and authorities," the Bible says in Titus 3:1–2, "to be obedient, to be ready to do whatever is good, to slander no one, to be peaceable and considerate, and to show true humility toward all men."

Talent on Loan from God

Finally, after discussing the need to speak the truth in a respectful and loving way, Jesus might turn to one of the most often quoted assertions that Limbaugh makes about himself: "I have talent on loan from God."

Although Limbaugh makes this claim with a self-congratulatory arrogance and puffed-up self-confidence, that might be overlooked as just being part of his comedy shtick and show biz persona. In fact, Limbaugh's friends describe him as being humble, gentle, and even painfully insecure when the microphone and TV lights click off.

But what about the claim itself? After all, Jesus would know for sure—*does* he have talent loaned from God?

"Rush, you're not exaggerating—God *has* given you talent, and a lot of it," Jesus would say. "But you need to know this: You're responsible for developing it and maximizing its impact."

You see, in addition to the fact that all human ability is a divine gift, 1 Corinthians 12:7 teaches that God loans a special species of talent to every one of His followers as a way of helping "the common good."

The biblical term for this is a "spiritual gift," a God-given ability to serve His kingdom in a way that transcends natural capabilities. Some have a gift of evangelism, others mercy, still others, administration, teaching, leadership, or various other gifts. It's through the interconnected use of these talents that God advances His church, and through His church, He grows His kingdom in the world.

But here's the snag: according to *U.S. News & World Report*, Limbaugh seldom attends church. And he isn't the only one who spends Sundays doing something else. Studies have shown that unchurched people almost unanimously believe that they can be good Christians independent of any religious institution, apparently subscribing to the cliché that they can worship God better while walking in the woods than sitting inside a building. And here's what's truly amazing: Two-thirds of *churchgoing* people agree!

Even so, the Bible doesn't envision—much less endorse—the idea of Lone Ranger Christians. Hebrews 10:25 is unambiguous: "Let us not give up meeting together, as some are in the habit of doing."

In the New Testament, active membership in a church is assumed. Actually the Bible describes two kinds of church members. People become "positional members" of Christ's universal church when they make the decision to follow Him. Then the

Bible invariably shows these Christians becoming "participating members" in a local body of believers.

Spiritual Free Agents

When we choose instead to act as spiritual free agents, we're cheating ourselves. The church is where we can grow deeper in our faith; increase our understanding of Scripture; offer thanks and worship to God; further develop a Christ-honoring world view; encourage, challenge, and care for each other; and strategically infiltrate the world with Christ's love and compassion. Apart from the church's consistent influence, it's too easy for our faith to atrophy and for us to fall prey to distorted teachings and hardened attitudes.

But there's another angle that's often overlooked: When we stay away, we're also cheating the church. God has loaned us talent for a purpose, and when we withhold it from what Jesus considers the most important and revolutionary institution in the world—which He lovingly refers to as His "bride"—we're robbing His kingdom.

What about you? Are you part of the problem of the church's declining influence in our society, or part of the solution? It may take some work to find the specific church that God wants for you, but it's worth the effort and commitment to make the search and then get involved.

Now, admittedly, many churches are bogged down in mediocrity and irrelevancy. I once vowed that I'd never get involved in a church because I thought I'd end up sitting on some mind-numbing committee that would haggle for months over what color the hymnal covers ought to be.

But when I got a taste of a ministry that has a dynamic, strategic, God-directed vision for impacting lives, and which offers a deep sense of community where people really care about each other, I couldn't get enough of it. I knew that whatever I invested there would yield monumental dividends that would never fade. And believe me—churches like that are just waiting for a person exactly like you to join their team and become a difference-maker.

After all, look at government, business, industry, schools, the media—as much good as they do, none of them holds the ultimate answers to life. God's church does, and part of the great adventure of Christianity is being a player in His movement to extend that influence into every nook and cranny of the world.

When I see firsthand the way God can turn a life inside out—like the way he transformed one of my friends from being a street gang leader steeped in violence into an inner-city youth worker serving kids out of love—I have to ask, "Who wouldn't want to deploy their talent in God's primary change-agent for the world?"

So on a personal and spiritual level, the church can help Rush Limbaugh, and in using his spiritual gift, Rush Limbaugh can help Christ's work through the church. And, of course, his radio and TV programs give him a rare opportunity to influence America. Christians should be praying that he would use that power not only to speak the truth but also to do it in love.

There's no question that Limbaugh knows what God can do. "I don't want any praise when I say this, but the primary influence on my life is Almighty God," he said in a magazine interview. "Without God's influence in life, nothing else matters."

That, Jesus would say, is the kind of message his listeners need to hear him speak—and to watch him live.

4

What Jesus Would Say to *Mother Teresa*

The first time I encountered what Mother Teresa calls "the poorest of the poor" was in 1987. At the time I was a volunteer for a ministry serving the needy in Southeast India, and I was on my way for a visit when our team stopped in Bombay.

We hired a taxi driver, telling him, "We don't want to see the Bombay they show on postcards. Take us to the *real* Bombay."

And he did. But despite my years of exploring the seamier side of life as a newspaper reporter, I wasn't prepared for *this*.

Lining the highway in this noisy, congested area of the city were small cardboard and burlap hovels, one after the other as far as the eye could see. They were situated right next to the road, where buses and cars spewed exhaust and soot. Each family had a six-by-six-foot hut, with perhaps a cardboard box as a table and, if they were lucky, a mat to sleep on.

There was an oppressive stench from the open sewage ditch that snaked through the area. Naked children roamed aimlessly, defecating in the ditch's polluted water. People with missing limbs or bodies contorted by deformities sat passively on the sidewalk. There were pink dogs running around, their fur totally scratched off. Insects buzzed everywhere.

It was a horrific scene—a place, the cab driver explained, where people are born on the sidewalk, live their lives on the sidewalk, and die on the sidewalk.

We were driving with the windows down so I could shoot photographs as we passed. More than anything, I wanted the cab just to keep moving. But we got stuck in traffic, and before I knew what was happening, the face of a little boy appeared in my window, just six inches away from me. He looked about the same age as my son, Kyle.

I was startled. It was one thing to view this ghastly scene through the lens of a camera; it was a whole different matter to come face-to-face with a ten-year-old youngster. He was scrawny and malnourished. His hair was filthy and matted. One eye was half closed; the other stared vacantly. There was blood oozing from scabs on his face.

He extended his hand and mumbled something in Hindi, apparently begging for coins. But his voice was a dull, lifeless monotone, as if he didn't expect any response. As if he had been drained of hope.

It was the first time I had ever seen such stark poverty up close—and I froze. I didn't know how to react. I was horrified and repulsed and overwhelmed to the point of paralysis.

I stammered that I didn't have any coins. That was true, although I did have a wallet crammed with Indian bills that were worth $1.60 each. But everyone had told me that you're only supposed to toss a few coins to beggars. "Just a few coins," they'd say. So I kept repeating, "I don't have any coins; I don't have any coins," and the boy kept mumbling in his monotone.

I broke out in a sweat. I just wanted the cab to get out of there, but it seemed like we were stuck forever. Finally, we started moving again. The driver reached out to push the boy away from the car, and he sort of stumbled. As we pulled away, I looked out the rear window and saw the disheartened youngster get swallowed up by the crowd—and that's when it hit me: the verse of Scripture where Jesus said, "Whatever you did for one of the least of these brothers of mine, you did for me" (Matt. 25:40).

And I felt like crying.

There's no way I could have done anything about the massive slums of Bombay, but I had a chance to do something—*anything*—to help this one little boy. Could I have given him a meal? Could I have gotten him the medical attention he obviously needed? Could I have bought him a pair of shoes? I could have radically improved his life, but my only response was to fumble and make excuses and to coldly offer no help at all.

In the backseat of that taxi on February 4, 1987, I prayed: "Lord, forgive me for letting You down. Forgive me for hoarding the love You've given to me instead of passing it on to others. Please, Lord, when I see a person in need—help me to see Your face."

To this day, if I close my eyes I can still picture that little boy. His face is imprinted in my memory. And my encounter with him riveted home that verse of Scripture in a way that changed my perspective forever.

The incident also gave me a deep appreciation for the way that same verse has been the driving force for Mother Teresa since 1948, when she started caring for the poorest of the poor in a place Rudyard Kipling called "The Big Calcutta Stink."

"My God, You, Only You"

Raised in Yugoslavia, Agnes Bojaxhiu decided when she was only twelve years old that she was going to become a nun. She left home at eighteen and studied in Darjeeling, India, where she joined the Loreto Sisters. For the following twenty years, she taught at St. Mary's High School, which was attended primarily by middle-class children. Asked to describe her, her colleagues often used the word "average."

It was on a train in 1946 that she felt God was calling her to serve the poor in the slums of India. "Soon after leaving Loreto, I was on the street, with no shelter, no company, no helper, no money, no employment, no promise, no guarantee, no security," she said. "Then I prayed, 'My God, You, only You. I trust in Your call, Your inspiration. You will not let me down.'"

She started by picking up one dying woman—who had been partly eaten by rats and ants in the gutter—and taking her to a hospital. Mother Teresa refused to budge until the reluctant doctors agreed to treat her. Then she talked the city into giving her space in a former Hindu temple, which she turned into a home for the dying.

Since then tens of thousands have been rescued off the streets. She has started facilities for lepers, orphans, and AIDS victims, and they've spread around the globe, from Ethiopia to Peru to Mexico to New York City.

Ever since she won the Nobel Peace Prize in 1979, the name Mother Teresa has become synonymous with servanthood, and that's the theme I want to focus on. Certainly we view some theological issues from different perspectives, but instead of focusing on those, I want to explore the way she exemplifies servanthood.

Because, let's face it, she has intrigued the entire world by showing that Christian servanthood can bring the kind of fulfillment that has eluded people who have so desperately sought satisfaction through serving themselves. Christians reap unexpected rewards and benefits that come not just from performing good deeds, but from doing so in the name of Jesus. As we'll see, there's a big difference.

The Greatest Reward

The title of this chapter is What Jesus Would Say to Mother Teresa, and I believe that what He would say—the very words themselves—would be her greatest reward. His response to a person with the faith and compassion of a servant can be found in Matthew 25:34–40:

> "Then the King will say to those on his right, 'Come, you who are blessed by my Father; take your inheritance, the kingdom prepared for you since the creation of the world. For I was hungry and you gave me something to eat, I was thirsty and you gave me something to drink, I was a stranger and you invited me in, I needed clothes and you clothed me, I was sick and you looked after me, I was in prison and you came to visit me.'
> "Then the righteous will answer him, 'Lord, when did we see you hungry and feed you, or thirsty and give you something to drink? When did we see you a stranger

and invite you in, or needing clothes and clothe you? When did we see you sick or in prison and go to visit you?'

"The King will reply, 'I tell you the truth, whatever you did for one of the least of these brothers of mine, you did for me.'"

I think Jesus would say to Mother Teresa: "*Thank you.* Thank you for the way you served Me as you served the poorest of the poor. For the way you washed Me when I was a leper, for the way you comforted Me when I was dying, for the way you cuddled Me as an abandoned infant, for the way you educated Me as an orphan, for the way you lovingly listened to Me when I was lonely. When you served each of those people, you were serving Me."

Wouldn't that be awe-inspiring to hear from the ultimate servant Himself? Think of the times in your life when you extended His grace to people in need—the times you gave money to help the needy, the times you participated in ministries that alleviated suffering, the times you spontaneously shared with someone desperate for help.

Now think of the moment of hearing Jesus say, "Thank you. When you served those people, you were serving Me in disguise." That's the most satisfying reward of all!

In fact, the longer I live as a follower of Jesus, the more that becomes the central motivation of my life. I long to hear Jesus say the words, "Well done, good and faithful servant."

What Makes a Mother Teresa?

There are other benefits to authentic Christian servant-hood, too. There's the kind of fulfillment that was evident even to a hard-nosed journalist who traveled to India years ago to see Mother Teresa and her colleagues in action.

"Their life is tough and austere by worldly standards," he wrote, "but I have never in my life met such delightful, happy servants, or seen such an atmosphere of absolute joy as they create."

Think about that for a moment—*that joy is being experienced in the midst of the Big Calcutta Stink!* What kind of fuel could these servants be running on? And how can *we* get some?

We can get that answer by taking a look at what makes a Mother Teresa a Mother Teresa. In other words, what makes her more than just a social worker who prays?

After all, Christians don't have a corner on the servanthood market. People who aren't Christians do a lot of nice things for the poor, too. Before I was a Christian, I gave to the United Way, I slipped a few coins into the Salvation Army kettle at Christmas, I donated old clothes to Goodwill. I bet a lot of non-Christians give to disaster relief funds, help fill sandbags at flood sites, and volunteer to repair houses battered by hurricanes. Lots of social workers help people, as do humanitarians and people who dabble in volunteerism.

All of that's fine, but there's something *different* about Mother Teresa, isn't there? And I don't mean just her; I'm referring to all the servant-minded Christians she represents.

There's something unique about why and how an authentic Christian serves others. It isn't a sporadic good deed here and there to work off middle-class guilt; it's a lifestyle that brings a level of satisfaction, adventure, effectiveness, and even longevity of service that many others don't seem to have.

So what would Jesus say are some of the qualities that distinguish His servants—like Mother Teresa—from others? Let's take a look at some key characteristics.

If you're a Christ-follower, you might want to use this checklist to see if these qualities are true for you. If you're a spiritual seeker, think about how these characteristics might open the door to the kind of otherwise inexplicable fulfillment that the journalist described in India—the kind of personal satisfaction you may have been looking for yourself.

Mother Teresa is not a manufacturer, but a distributor.

In his book *On Being a Servant of God*, author Warren Wiersbe offers a helpful distinction between servants who are *manufacturers* and those who are *distributors*.

You see, some people manufacture their compassion for the needy out of whatever is motivating them. For instance, maybe they're feeling guilty over their own affluence. Perhaps they pity the poor or altruistically sense they should give something back to the world. Maybe they have a neurotic drive to put the needs of others before their own in order to make themselves feel worthwhile. Whatever the source, they have to create their compassion and, sooner or later, it's probably going to run out.

However, Mother Teresa isn't primarily a manufacturer but a distributor. In other words every morning she spends time connecting with God in prayer, meditating on the sacrifice He made on her behalf, drinking in His love from the Bible, and reminding herself of His grace. Then during the day she merely acts as a conduit to channel that compassion to others.

In fact, the more she empties herself in serving others, the more room there is for God to fill her back up. And, of course, God's supply of compassion never runs dry.

It keeps servanthood fresh for the long haul when you know your primary role as a Christian isn't just to do a bunch of good deeds, but it's to stay connected with God and give away the love He gives you.

Mother Teresa likes to use the analogy of electricity. "The wire is you and me; the current is God," she says. "We have the power to let the current pass through us, use us, and produce the light of the world—Jesus."

She isn't serving herself, but she's serving God.

For some people serving others is really a thinly disguised form of self-promotionalism. One writer said this about one of the big trends of the 1990s—volunteerism:

> There's so much to gain personally from volunteering. You feel good. You see and learn things you otherwise wouldn't have. You test your abilities. You often find yourself rubbing shoulders with pillars of the community who can help your business or career. Volunteering can be yet another path to upward mobility.

That sounds like a repackaging of the "me-ism" of the 1980s, doesn't it? Yet the Bible says in Philippians 2:3, "Do nothing out of selfish ambition or vain conceit."

The problem is that when your main goal is to feed your own satisfaction, you're always going to feel hungry for more. But with Mother Teresa, the satisfaction she receives is a by-product of loving Jesus through her servanthood. He's the one who said that whatever she does for the least among us, she's doing for Him, and that motivates her. Why? Because she loves God!

In fact, someone once said to Mother Teresa, "I wouldn't touch a leper for a thousand dollars."

"Neither would I," she replied. "But I would willingly tend him for the love of God."

Here's the point: Her servanthood knits her closer and closer to the Jesus she's serving, and it's that intimate and loving proximity to Him that brings her fulfillment.

She doesn't pity the people she serves, but she respects them.

This is a very significant distinction. You see, if a person is serving someone else because he feels sorry for him or pities him or is trying to fulfill some kind of obligation, that attitude tends to bleed through and the needy person feels devalued. A subtle barrier develops between the servant and the person being served.

But Mother Teresa sees each person as being imprinted with God's image, and so every single individual has infinite value in her eyes. They're worthy of being treated with dignity and respect. "Our poor are very great people, very lovable people," she likes to say.

This mind-set takes the needy individual out of the realm of being a case number or a patient and opens the door to a real depth of community taking place between him and the servant. Christians discover great fulfillment in this kind of oneness.

She isn't just willing to serve, but she's willing to sacrifice.

On an episode of the *Seinfeld* television show, the main characters decided to jump on the volunteerism bandwagon by signing up to help some elderly people whose infirmities confined them to their apartments. It seemed like a 1990s thing to do—until serving became inconvenient or difficult. That's when, one by one, they dropped out of the volunteer program.

But Mother Teresa's attitude is, "It hurt Jesus to love us," and so she's willing to continue to serve others even when it costs her. She gives more than just out of her surplus, like the woman in Luke 21 who offered two small copper coins to the temple. Jesus praised her gift as being the greatest because while others gave out of their abundance, she gave all she had.

Jesus set the standard for us through His own "downward mobility" and sacrificial servanthood: "My command is this: Love each other as I have loved you" (John 15:12).

Her agenda isn't her own, but it's God's.

Through prayer Mother Teresa is attuned to God's guidance for her life. For instance, it was His distinct leading that prompted her to leave the relative comfort of teaching high school and go to the slums of Calcutta.

"I felt that God wanted from me something more," she said in *My Life for the Poor.* "He wanted me to be poor with the poor and to love Him in the distressing disguise of the poorest of the poor."

It's a terrific source of strength when you're certain you're following what God wants for your life. In fact, I believe that one reason Mother Teresa has persevered and thrived is that during times of turbulence—when most people would have jumped ship—she had the anchor of being firmly convinced that she is precisely where God wants her to be.

She doesn't just have ability, but she has a spiritual gift.

All of us have some abilities, and they can carry us a certain distance. But the Bible says in 1 Corinthians 12:7 that every follower of Jesus is given one or more spiritual gifts, which are God-given abilities to serve in a way that exceeds natural talent.

Several gifts are listed in the Bible. Here's a definition of the spiritual gift of mercy: "It's the divine enablement to minister cheerfully and appropriately to people who are suffering." That's Mother Teresa in a sentence!

One explanation for why she's so effective and fulfilled is because she's doing exactly what God has wired her up to do and what He enables her to do through the activation of her gifts by the Holy Spirit. That's an advantage non-Christians just don't have.

67

Of course, not every Christian has this particular spiritual gift. For example, it's not in the mix that God has given to me. But all Christians are called to express compassion to those in need, and God will provide us with the grace we need to be able to do that.

She doesn't rely on an organization, but she relies radically on God.

There's a story about the time Mother Teresa said to her superiors, "I have five pennies and a dream from God to build an orphanage."

Her superiors looked at each other and then said to her, "Well, Mother Teresa, you can't build an orphanage with five pennies. With five pennies, you can do nothing."

"I know," she replied. "But with *God* and five pennies, I can do *anything*."

This is what puts the adventure in following Jesus! God built that orphanage as He has built the rest of her ministry because she has been radically dependent on Him. She receives no church support, no governmental subsidies, and she offers no salaries—but God has come through time after time and she has never had to turn away a needy person.

She relates an incident about the chairman of a large Indian corporation who came to donate some property in Bombay. First he asked, "Mother, how is your work financed?"

She said, "Mr. Thomas, who sent you here?"

"Well," he replied, "I felt an urge inside of me."

"Other people like you come to see me and say the same thing," she said. "*That* is my budget."

She has recounted story after story about how God has come through for her in amazing ways. Like the time when there was no more bread to give the poor—until, out of the blue, two trucks pulled up and dumped enough bread to feed everyone at the facility for several days. It seems that the schools in Calcutta had unexpectedly closed for the day, and someone suggested donating the lunch bread to Mother Teresa.

Another time a coworker at another facility called her to ask for 50,000 rupees to start a children's home. Mother Teresa said she didn't have the money but would pray about it.

As soon as she hung up, the phone rang again. "You've just won an award from the Philippines," a newspaper reporter said.

"How much is it?" she asked.

"Fifty thousand rupees."

She called back her colleague. "You have your orphanage," she said.

You can try to dismiss these events as coincidence, but that's hard to do when they happen time after time. That's the kind of adventure that comes with radical reliance on God.

She isn't concerned just about today, but she has an eye on eternity.

How much good does it do to help a person die in comfort without ever telling him how he can be comforted by Christ through all eternity?

The ultimate expression of love is to clearly communicate how Christ is the only hope for heaven, and that salvation cannot be earned but must be received as a gift from God. That must be the message of any authentic Christian ministry. "Watch your life and doctrine closely," the apostle Paul cautioned in 1 Timothy 4:16.

It's that reality of eternity hanging in the balance that gives a compelling sense of urgency, supreme meaning, and utmost importance to serving in the name of Christ.

"If we really love God, we cannot but be consumed with the desire of saving souls, the greatest and dearest interest of Jesus," Mother Teresa says. Her approach is this: "We preach Christ without preaching—not by words, but by putting His love and our love into living action." And that can be powerful, as long as the message gets through.

Mother Teresa tells the story of an atheist who came one day to her home for the dying. A sickly, maggot-covered man had just been brought in from the gutters, and some volunteers were bathing and caring for him, unaware that the atheist was watching.

Later he said, "I came here godless. I came here full of hatred. I am going full of God. I have seen God's love in action. I have seen that through the hands of that sister, through her face, through her tenderness—so full of love for that man. *Now I believe.*"

She also described how a Muslim cleric watched for the longest time as her volunteers washed a leper. "All these years, I have believed that Jesus was a prophet," he said afterward. "But today I believe Jesus Christ is God, if He is able to give such joy to this sister, enabling her to do her work with so much love."

Mother Teresa is onto something, isn't she? She's found that authentic Christian servanthood—fueled by God's love and compassion—can be so powerful that just witnessing it can help turn an unbeliever to Christ. That's potent stuff!

"Let your light shine before men, that they may see your good deeds and praise your Father in heaven," Jesus said in Matthew 5:16.

What Mother Teresa Would Say

This sort of life-changing servanthood isn't merely trendy volunteerism or conscience-soothing good deeds. It's servanthood with a difference. It's servanthood that flows out of a flourishing relationship with Christ, that's dependent on Him, that's empowered by Him, and that's guided by Him. It's serving others as we would serve Jesus Himself.

And it brings an abundance of rewards. Said Jesus in Luke 6:38: "Give, and it will be given to you. A good measure, pressed down, shaken together and running over, will be poured into your lap. For with the measure you use, it will be measured to you."

So if you feel tugged toward serving others in the name of Christ, what should you do? Should you rush out to buy a one-way ticket to Calcutta? How would Mother Teresa suggest that someone get started? In other words let's turn the tables and ask what Mother Teresa might say to us.

Actually, we don't have to guess because she's been asked that question many times before. Here's the response she has given:

> I know you think you should make a trip to Calcutta, but I strongly advise you to save your airfare and spend it on the poor in your own country. It's easy to love people far away. It's not always easy to love those who

live right next to us. There are thousands of people dying for a piece of bread, but there are thousands more dying for a bit of love or a bit of acknowledgment.

The truth is that the worst disease today is not leprosy or tuberculosis; it's being unwanted, it's being left out, it's being forgotten. The greatest scourge is to be so suffocated with things that we forget the next person.

She talks about coming to the affluent West and visiting a beautifully decorated nursing home, but finding all the residents sitting in wheelchairs facing the door. "Why are all these people looking toward the door?" she asked. "Why aren't they smiling? I'm used to seeing smiles on all our people, even the dying ones."

"It's like this every day," the nurse replied. "They're always hoping somebody will come and visit them. Their loneliness is eating them up."

My guess is that Mother Teresa would ask us: "*Who's staring at the door, waiting for a person like you?*"

Maybe it's somebody under your own roof—a son or daughter who's secretly aching to talk about things that are deep in their soul. Maybe it's an elderly parent or grandparent who feels discarded, or the guy at work who's always the odd man out, or the child who's shunned by fellow students. Or the former friend whose calls you don't return anymore, or the single mom whose life is collapsing in on her.

Perhaps it's the neighbor who's steeped in despair, or the widow whose relational world has shrunk to nothing, or the immigrant who feels isolated and lonely in a confusing new culture. Or your employee who's struggling with personal problems, or the person in your ministry who seems troubled by something.

Do you know someone who's staring at the door, waiting for a person like you? Even as I write this, I do.

I think Mother Teresa would say to all of us, "Go to them and practice. Practice being a distributor of God's compassion. Practice honoring them as a person engraved with the image of God. Practice meeting their needs. Practice encouraging them. Practice listening to them. *Pretend you're doing it for Jesus. Because, in a very real sense, you are.*"

"*I tell you the truth,*" said Jesus. "*Whatever you did for one of the least of these brothers of mine, you did for me.*"

5

What Jesus Would Say to *Michael Jordan*

Until he turned thirty, Michael Jordan's basketball career kept soaring into the stratosphere. He attained victory after victory; set record after record; achieved one world championship, then a second, and finally a third—and he savored greater and greater rewards and adulation in an uninterrupted string of heady accomplishments.

He was a single-handed economic boom. Experts calculated that his superstar magnetism was worth $1 *billion* to Chicago's regional economy because of increased tourism and other spin-offs.

He was the king of cash flow. His income approached $100,000 *per day*, enough money every year to stretch in dollar bills from New York to San Francisco—and beyond.

He was the most successfully marketed athlete in history. His endorsements boosted the bottom line of Nike shoes, McDonald's hamburgers, Chevrolet cars, and Hanes underwear. In fact, when he started publicly gulping Gatorade, sales of the thirst-quencher squirted up twenty percent.

He was the most famous athlete on the planet. For years, when Chicagoans went overseas and told people where they were from, foreigners would chant "Al Capone! Al Capone!" and pretend to fire a machine gun. But now, when Chicagoans reveal where they're from, people grin and respond, "Michael Jordan! Michael Jordan! You get me poster?"

He was the most imitated individual in America. Kids on playgrounds everywhere were striving to "be like Mike" by trying to stuff a basketball with gravity-defying leaps and artistic aplomb, their tongues wagging in reverent mimicry.

Most of all, Michael Jeffrey Jordan was a ballet dancer with a basketball, capable of a forty-eight-inch vertical jump with astounding grace. Marveled one coach: "When God decided to create the perfect basketball player and send him down here, He gave him to the Jordans."

The Jordans, James and Deloris, both children of share-croppers, raised Michael and his four siblings in what one biographer called "a vibrant Christian home." The family faithfully attended an African Methodist Episcopal Church. As for sports, the Jordans never missed any of Michael's high school or college basketball games and frequently cheered his exploits with the Chicago Bulls. It was James Jordan who wrapped his arm around his son as he tearfully hugged his first world championship trophy.

Then came Michael Jordan's thirtieth year. That's when his life was forever altered by three headline-grabbing events. First, there were embarrassing allegations over his gambling. Second, there was the heartbreaking murder of his father. And third was his world-stunning decision to quit basketball at the apex of his career.

It must have been dizzying to endure those gut-wrenching experiences in such a short span of time, especially under the spotlight of public scrutiny. Yet at all three of those personal turning points, I believe Jesus would have whispered to Michael Jordan the same thing He would say to you and me when the circumstances of life seem overwhelming: *"I'm here for you."*

Let's see how that would play out in each of these three areas of challenge.

What's Driving Michael?

By all accounts, Michael Jordan loves to wager. He'll aggressively bet on a game of H-O-R-S-E, a hand of cards, or a round of golf. Increasingly during his basketball career, allegations of excessive gambling began to pester him. Then came publication of the book *Michael & Me*, in which golfing partner Richard Esquinas accused Jordan of losing $1.25 million to him. Esquinas admitted he's a compulsive gambler and speculated about Jordan: "I wonder if he has much more of a problem with gambling than I do."

Jordan didn't deny he bet on golf games with Esquinas, but said the $1.25 million amount was "preposterous." His dad said Jordan doesn't have a gambling problem but conceded that he does, indeed, have an addiction—to competition.

It's an addiction that apparently pushed him into a corner where he felt compelled to deceive. When the government found a $57,000 check from Jordan in the bank account of a convicted felon, he first told his fans it was a loan to build a driving range. But under oath at the man's trial, Jordan reversed himself by admitting the money was to pay off golf and card debts.

Authorities also found photocopies of $108,000 in Jordan's checks in the briefcase of a bail bondsman who had been murdered. The victim's lawyer said the money, in part, was paid to cover gambling debts.

The National Basketball Association appointed a former judge to investigate, and Jordan told him there were no more large gambling debts that could embarrass himself or the league. But a few months later came Esquinas's allegations. In the words of *Sports Illustrated*, "He had clearly been caught in another lie."

And then there was Jordan's late-night trip to Atlantic City to gamble in the midst of a crucial playoff road trip. The escapade made headlines and prompted Jordan to temporarily freeze out the media in retaliation for their coverage.

Nobody knows what it is about gambling that's so alluring to Jordan. One gambling expert said that, in general, it's the action, the excitement, the competitiveness, the on-the-edge risk-taking that really "juices" gamblers. And certainly Jordan is attracted to competition.

"There may be no more brutally competitive person alive," wrote *Men's Journal* in a profile on Jordan. "Competitiveness is Jordan's addiction, a hunger that made him stunningly better and better each of his nine seasons in the NBA."

Taking a Gamble on God

How would Jesus react to the gambling issue? With, I believe, more compassion than condemnation, more grace-filled concern than shaming criticism. After all, part of the Bible's distaste for wagering comes from God's loving attempt to safeguard us from sliding into self-defeating situations where we turn to lies or other wrongdoing to try to extricate ourselves from our losses. In the end God has our best interests at heart.

"Michael," Jesus might say, "I want to protect you from having your healthy competitiveness become an unhealthy compulsion. Let Me help you peer inside of yourself to get at the root of what's driving you toward the edge."

I believe Jesus would make that same offer to those whose positive desire to work has degenerated into a destructive pattern of workaholism, or to those whose healthy interest in sex has become an unhealthy excursion into promiscuity or pornography, or to those whose repeated risk-taking has escalated into a reckless cry for help.

Sometimes dynamics in our past twist us into a knot of self-destructive behavior which we can't seem to untangle on our own. And as we compulsively fall victim to wrongful conduct over and over, sometimes we become increasingly embarrassed about going back to God for forgiveness. We become afraid that at some point He'll exclaim, "Look, enough is enough!" So we cut ourselves off from the very One who can help us the most.

But Jesus is waiting for us to cry out to Him for help because He's anxious to respond. His mercy, the Bible proclaims, is fresh every morning. There's no debt of wrongdoing that we can submit to Him for forgiveness that He'll ship back to us with the words "Insufficient Funds" stamped on it.

And beyond forgiving us, He can heal us. Just as He often chooses to restore us physically through a surgeon's skills, He may choose to heal us through a minister or Christian counselor who can help us use biblical truth to unravel the dysfunction of our past that's got us so tied up in self-damaging conduct.

In fact, if you're inexplicably drawn to a pattern of wrong-doing in your life and you're sort of waiting for someone to give you permission to see a Christian counselor, let me be the one to do it right now. *You have permission.* Let God heal your tomorrows by applying the Bible-based insights of a godly counselor to the difficulties of your past.

What God Might Say to *Us*

I think Jesus might have something else to say about those gambling episodes. During the height of the issue, I heard people tsk-tsking Jordan with a very self-righteous attitude. "What a waste!" they'd say. "Think of the number of people who could have been helped with that money he lost in gambling."

And while that's true—and it's something Jordan must face—I think Jesus might turn to *us* and ask how many of *our* resources do *we* let slip through *our* fingers through sloppy management? How much do we spend on luxury items that we don't really need? How many superfluous options do we order for our new cars? How many expensive shirts or dresses do we buy on the spur-of-the-moment but which end up hanging unused in the back of our too-full closets? As a percentage of our income, we may actually be wasting more than Jordan lost through his gambling. But the amount isn't the point.

The Bible teaches that all we have—whether it's a little or a lot—belongs to God because He's the one who enabled us to earn it. And, ironically, we're robbing ourselves when we handle our resources so casually that some of them slip away. We miss the soul satisfaction that can come when we conscientiously and strategically leverage our wealth to express God's compassion to the world.

I remember one summer evening when my seventeen-year-old daughter, Alison, was daydreaming at dinner. "What are you thinking about?" I asked.

"Oh," she said. "Remember last Christmas when our small group at church got together and pooled our allowances and sort of adopted that family? She was a single mom, and she didn't have much of anything, so we bought her kids food and presents and we threw a big party for them in their apartment. I was just sitting here thinking: *That really meant a lot to me.*"

God has used that sacrificial experience to give Alison a rich memory that she'll treasure the rest of her life. But when I was her age, I wasted most of my allowance on things that didn't really matter. And as an adult I'm not always as prudent with my finances as I should be. I honor God much more—and I experience the kind of reward that Alison was feeling—when I scrupulously manage my resources so I can liberally share some of them with people in need.

How about you? As you look at your finances, are there ways you can plug some unnecessary leaks and then use those funds to extend God's grace to a person, a family, or a worthy organization? Or, for example, can you commit to having a brown-bag lunch one extra day a week so you can save the money you would have spent at a restaurant and mail it anonymously to a single mom who's struggling to survive?

I think Jesus would echo to Michael Jordan—and to you and me—what wealthy King Solomon wrote in Proverbs 19:17: "He who is kind to the poor lends to the LORD, and he will reward him for what he has done."

What a great perspective to have—when we bless the poor with our resources and time, we can picture ourselves actually giving to God Himself. And as my daughter Alison discovered, there's no better reward than basking in God's approval when we serve the needy in His name.

As it turned out, the controversy over Michael Jordan's gambling was a nagging distraction for him and his team as they successfully fought to clinch their third consecutive world championship in 1993. But Jordan's next turning point, which came just a couple of months later, proved much more devastating.

A Father and Best Friend

The ritual took place before every Chicago Bulls game that Michael Jordan's parents were planning to attend. In the locker room, suiting up, Jordan had to satisfy himself that his parents were in their seats. "I feel I have to make sure that they're there safely," he told writer Bob Greene. "I have to check before the game, just so I know."

Unable to show his face in the stadium without causing a commotion, Jordan would dispatch someone to determine if his parents had arrived and then come back and report to him. "I've been doing that ever since high school," he explained. "It's just a sense of safety, I guess."

Then, referring to his father, he added: "When he's there, I know I have at least one fan."

Michael Jordan's dad was more than a father to him. He was his best friend. A confidante. A coach. A fan during cold spells as well as hot streaks. In fact, it was "Pops," as he was called, who inspired Michael's memorable habit of hanging out his tongue as he launched himself on his patented slam-dunks. You see, Pops tended to expose his tongue while he was concentrating on fixing his car with young Michael at his side, watching admiringly and handing him tools.

And then came the senseless violence that ended James Jordan's life on a lonely North Carolina roadside in August 1993. Apparently a robbery victim, Jordan had been shot in the chest and his car stolen and stripped. His body was discarded in a river.

The crime was all the more shocking because it exposed the truth that even Michael Jordan's wealth and fame couldn't insulate his family from the realities of a sin-scarred world. And if someone like Michael Jordan can't protect his family from America's escalating violence, who can? We move to "safe" neighborhoods, we buy burglar alarms, we put "The Club" on our car, we may even think our spirituality will protect us. But in the end the world's sin is pervasive.

Jesus made that clear in talking with His followers, warning them: "In the world you have tribulation" (John 16:33 NASB).

How can anyone argue with that? In fact, we could divide the world into two groups—those who have already faced a tragedy in their lives, and those who will. There are no exceptions.

But fortunately Jesus didn't stop with just a *prediction* of trouble—He also offered a *prescription* for dealing with it. Here's the entire verse, because I think it's what Jesus might very well say to Michael Jordan in the midst of his personal turmoil: "These things I have spoken to you, that in Me you may have peace. In the world, you have tribulation, but take courage; I have overcome the world."

Peace and courage—aren't they what we crave when the bottom falls out of life? Don't we need courage to face the future? And don't we desire a comforting sense of peace that passes human understanding?

Michael Jordan recognized that in his own way. At a memorial service for his father, he gave a brief eulogy but broke down in tears before he could finish. His mother stood and embraced him. Afterward Jordan made this comment to reporters: "With the help of God's strength, I will find the inner peace to carry on."

How can Michael Jordan—and how can we—access this courage and peace of God? As I've searched for the answer to that question in my own life, I've found some lessons in the stories of three people named Judy, Ignatius, and Ray.

Peace and Courage

As a newspaper reporter, I frequently dealt with crime victims and their relatives. And I often saw death. I've looked into people's eyes when it was dawning on them that they weren't going to make it through the night. And I've seen instances when God has offered comfort and fortitude to people who were facing life's ultimate crisis.

In fact, one incident was so powerful that I'll never forget it. At the time I was doing a series of articles on the Ford Pinto controversy. You might remember the Pinto as the car that tended to blow up when it was hit from behind. Several people burned to death in Pintos, and the question was whether Ford had marketed a car it knew was unreasonably dangerous.

As part of the investigation, I looked into a terrible Pinto accident in Indiana in which three teenage girls had been killed. They were slowing to a stop in their Pinto when they were hit from behind by a Chevy van, sparking an explosion that one witness likened to a napalm bomb going off. Two of the girls burned to death in a matter of moments, but the driver—an eighteen-year-old named Judy—was flung from the car. She was horribly burned over ninety-five percent of her body, yet somehow she was still alive.

They rushed her to a hospital, where doctors realized there was nothing anyone could do for her. They decided to send her by ambulance to a burn center about seventy-five miles away where she could be more comfortable. A nurse rode along with her.

Can you imagine how difficult that trip must have been? While Judy wasn't in a lot of physical pain because of damage to her nerve endings, she was in intense emotional distress. She was coming to realize that these were her last hours. She was separated from her family and friends. She was wracked by anxiety. I mean, what would you do if you were the nurse riding with her? What would you say when Judy asked, "I'm not ever going to have children, am I?"

The nurse said the trip started out as a nightmare because nothing could comfort Judy or ease her fear. At least, nothing until Judy mentioned something about Jesus, and the nurse realized that Judy was a Christian, as she was.

Now the nurse knew what to do. With tears running down her cheeks, she recited a Bible verse that turned out to be the only medication that could quiet Judy's fears and soothe her apprehensions. The words were from Isaiah 43:

Fear not, for I have redeemed you;
I have called you by name; you are mine.
When you pass through the waters,
I will be with you;
and when you pass through the rivers,
they will not sweep over you.
When you walk through the fire,
you will not be burned;
the flames will not set you ablaze.
For I am the LORD, your God,
the Holy One of Israel, your Savior.

Upon hearing that, Judy slowly began to take on a calmness and courage that carried her through the last difficult hours of her life. She just needed to be reminded of the truth that she belonged to God and that, ultimately, not even fire could destroy what is His.

Judy experienced peace because of God's promise that He would not abandon her, and she found courage because she had confidence that she would be with Him for eternity. Because Jesus had overcome the grave, so would she.

What about you? Where are you going to turn when you face the kind of crisis that nobody on earth can solve? What will you do when you can't pull any more strings and when your clout has no more influence? When a doctor's test brings bad news. When a drunk driver crosses the center line and hits your child's car. When the violence of the world strikes close to home. Or when you get a call like Michael Jordan did about his father.

When those times come—as Jesus said they surely will—we can collapse in our fear, or we can call out to a God who has the power and the inclination to help us.

Strength from Confidence

Courage and peace grow out of confidence—the assurance that Jesus is who He claimed to be and that He has the ability to fulfill His promises, including the stunning one in Romans 8:28 that says, "And we know that in all things God works for the good of those who love him, who have been called according to his purpose."

After all, lots of religious leaders can offer advice on how to cope when life deals us a disaster. But only Jesus has proven through His miraculous resurrection that He has supernatural power to make a difference in our lives. Jesus is uniquely qualified to help us because only He has overcome the world. When we have confidence in that truth, it bolsters our courage and peace.

Ignatius found that out personally. He lived in the first century, not long after Jesus walked the earth, and he became the leader of the church in the city of Antioch. Now this wasn't a very healthy occupation at the time. The modern equivalent would be Salman Rushdie hawking *Satanic Verses* in downtown Teheran. You see, back in Ignatius's day, the Roman government was determined to douse the Christian movement, which was spreading like wildfire despite persecution.

One day ten Roman soldiers broke into Ignatius's house, chained him up, and carted him off to Rome. His fate was clear—unless he renounced Jesus Christ, he would be tortured with fire and torn apart by wild animals.

That kind of threat would quickly put an end to religious game-playing, wouldn't it? Did he *really* have confidence in Christ? Was he certain enough to bet his very life on Him? I can imagine Ignatius taking time out to do a quick faith-check.

First, because he had been a Christ-follower for many decades, Ignatius would have been able to go down a personal checklist of Christ's faithfulness to him. Hadn't Jesus changed his life? Hadn't he seen how Jesus transformed the lives of others? When Ignatius had reached out during lesser crises, hadn't Jesus proven trustworthy again and again? "I put my confidence in the grace of Jesus Christ," he said.

And, second, Ignatius lived at a time when people were still alive who could confirm the reality of Christ's life, teachings, death, and resurrection. For instance, the apostle Paul reported that more than five hundred individuals saw the resurrected Jesus with their own eyes. Many of them, as well as the people they told, lived for years afterward and could provide personal accounts to anyone who asked what had happened.

"At the very least, any thinking person [among the perse-cuted early Christians] would make every possible effort to verify the accuracy of the Gospel reports," said author Josh McDowell. "From the very beginning, such a vast Christian network of mul-tiplication spread out across the [Roman] empire that it would have been easy enough to verify the historical events of Jesus' life. Even 120 years after the death of Christ, at least one godly Chris-tian, Polycarp, was still living who could verify what some of the original disciples of Jesus had reported."

History is clear that Ignatius talked with Polycarp. There's even some indication in church tradition that Ignatius was taught by the apostle John, an eyewitness to Christ's life and resurrec-tion. And Ignatius certainly would have been aware of the news that the apostles Peter and Paul had gone to their deaths main-taining that there had been no mistake—there had been no hallu-cinations or trickery. They had actually seen for themselves how Jesus overcame the grave.

"The foundation of faith for Ignatius," said McDowell, "was the undeniable historical facts of Jesus' birth, life, death, and bod-ily resurrection."

By the time Ignatius had to put his faith on the line, he didn't just have some vague or tenuous belief in Christ. He didn't halfheartedly mouth the Christian party line. Listen to the conviction that Ignatius displayed in one of the letters he wrote on his way to a brutal death in the Coliseum: "For myself, I am *convinced* and believe that after the resurrection [Jesus] was in the flesh."

In another letter he adamantly affirmed that Jesus "was *truly* born and ate and drank, was *truly* persecuted under Pontius Pilate, was *truly* crucified and died in the sight of those in heaven and on earth, and was *truly* raised from the dead, His Father having raised Him, who in the like fashion will so raise us also who believe on Him."

And he passionately urged others to be "fully persuaded" that Christ's death and resurrection weren't a myth or a mirage but they "*actually* and *assuredly*" took place.

These things *really* happened. They were events in history that skeptics could check out for themselves. For Ignatius, there was no ambiguity—and because of that, he faced death with a courage and peace that have amazed people throughout history. Thousands of others followed suit, and I'll tell you what—all of that has helped build my own confidence.

This Is Why I Believe

Now you might say it was easier for Ignatius to be confident because he lived at a time when the evidence about Christ was so fresh. But I knew a man who was like a modern Ignatius, except instead of being confronted by hostile soldiers, he was challenged by cynical teenagers.

His name was Ray, and he was a retired FBI agent who had been a leading expert on organized crime. He spent his entire career building airtight cases against mobsters and was well acquainted with what constituted reliable and convincing evidence.

One day he was talking about God with some teenagers in a youth prison, and they hit him with some tough questions: "Why do you believe that junk?" "How can you trust a book that's full of fairy tales?" "Isn't all of that stuff about Jesus just make-believe?"

Ray was shaken. Instead of feeling confident, he was confused. He wasn't exactly sure what he believed and why. So he decided to put his investigative skills to use. He went out and systematically checked the record of history, obtained answers to the questions, and got a tighter grip on exactly what he *really* believed and why he believed it.

He ended up putting together a fact-packed, fourteen-page summary of why he found the evidence for Christianity to be so convincing. Then he went back to the teenagers and placed it on the table, declaring: "Here! *This* is why I believe."

God used that experience to bolster Ray's confidence by strengthening the foundation of his faith. And it happened just in time, because shortly after that Ray was dealt a wild card. He was diagnosed with a virulent form of cancer.

I went to visit him in his home a few days before he died. Despite his pain, he was clearly a man who was resting in Christ's courage and peace. Though his voice was hoarse, there was a ring of confidence when he said: "Well, Lee, at least I *know* where I'm going."

Several times during those last days, his small-group members from church would form a semicircle around his bed and sing a worship chorus that had become Ray's theme. It's called "Fear Not," and its words are based on the same verses that the nurse had recited to Judy in that ambulance a dozen years earlier: *"Fear not, for I am with you, says the Lord. I have redeemed you, I have called you by name—child, you are mine!"*

Let me ask you this: When the time for game-playing stops, are you going to have a courage and peace built on confidence? Or are you still wrestling with exactly what you believe and why? Because if your mind isn't really sure what it believes, how can your heart fully embrace it?

Let me make two suggestions for bolstering your confidence. First, do what Ray did—systematically check out God. Shore up the foundation of your faith. Christian bookstores are stocked with many excellent books to help boost your certainty.

And, second, let God build a spiritual track record in your life. When I've been rocked by a crisis, I've gained great strength from looking back and seeing all the times God has been faithful to me. When you entrust God with control of your life and have an authentic relationship with Him, over time you compile irrefutable personal evidence of His trustworthiness. But in order for you to let God build that record, you need to be willing to yield the ongoing leadership of your life to Him.

As for Michael Jordan, he didn't talk much to the media about his father during his time of grieving. The loss was too painful for him. If you've wept at the funeral of a loved one, as I have, you can understand how he feels. If not, someday you will.

Even eight months after the slaying, Jordan told a reporter that his mind was often dominated by thoughts about his dad. "I think about him when I'm worried, and I think about him when I have a decision to make. I think about him when I have a bad problem." The wounds from such a loss take a long time to heal.

When you're faced with the kind of pain that no human being can relieve, remember the words of Jesus: "These things I have spoken to you, that in Me you may have peace. In the world you have tribulation, but take courage; I have overcome the world."

The Retirement that Shook the World

The news was more spectacular than a game-winning three-pointer at the buzzer. "Good-Bye to the Game" headlined *USA Today*. "Jordan's Decision Slams NBA," bannered the *Los Angeles Times*. His hometown newspaper, the *Chicago Tribune*, emblazoned this headline over a color portrait of Jordan: "So Long, Michael; It's Been Great."

On October 6, 1993, in the third world-stunning event of his thirtieth year, Jordan officially closed the book on the most illustrious basketball career of all time. The most famous athlete in the world picked up his ball and went home.

Predictably Nike's stock plummeted, but it promptly rebounded when people realized Jordan would remain its spokesman.

Nobody knows how much his father's death influenced Jordan's decision. He once said that if his parents weren't in the stands watching him play, "a part of me isn't there." And so maybe this move was inevitable. *Newsweek* quoted one coach who predicted the retirement as saying: "Who knows the psychological hurt he feels with the loss of his dad? With everything he's achieved, now with an emptiness and a void, why wouldn't

Michael ask himself, 'What's left?' and answer, quite logically, 'Nothing.'"

As for Jordan, he downplayed the connection, saying he would have retired even if his father were still alive. The real impetus, he said, came from elsewhere.

"I've always stressed to people who have known me . . . that when I lose the sense of motivation and the sense to prove something as a basketball player, it's time for me to move away from the game of basketball," he told the media. "I've reached the pinnacle of my career. I've achieved a lot in that short amount of time, if you want to call it short, but I just feel that I don't have anything else to prove to myself."

So what would Jesus say to Michael Jordan, who has accomplished so much at so young an age? I could imagine Him saying, "Michael, you've got the whole world at your feet, and that's great. But what you've achieved so far can be a prelude to even greater and more far-reaching accomplishments. Remember what the Bible says in Luke 12:48: 'Much is required from those to whom much is given, for their responsibility is greater'" (LB).

After all, God doesn't just prosper people with the idea that they'll live in luxury while the needs of others go unmet. Financial success carries an obligation to serve and help others out of a grateful heart for God's blessings. But here's the amazing thing: This can be one of the most exciting and fulfilling things you can ever do.

Warm-Up for the Main Event

As I was watching Michael Jordan on television a few months before his retirement, do you know what made him light up? It was when the reporter asked him about a program that Jordan was underwriting that will help one million disadvantaged sixth-grade students around the country to get a better education. *That's* what got him excited. You could hear it in his voice and see it on his face.

And friends say Jordan is becoming increasingly impassioned about his Michael Jordan Foundation, which supports charities that help children.

I think Jesus would say to Michael Jordan and everyone else who He has financially blessed: "I'm offering you a great opportunity to personally experience how My economy works: The more you give to others in need, the more you sacrifice out of what I've given you, the more you pour out your resources in response to the grace I've poured into your life, the more satisfaction I'll flow into your soul."

Think about this: What if Michael Jordan's phenomenal basketball career was just a warm-up to something even more dazzling? And I'm not talking about merely mastering baseball or some other sport. What if the world saw him as the man who gained the whole world but didn't lose his soul? What if he displayed such creative generosity and strategic giving that people would shake their heads in amazement and be inspired once again to "be like Mike"?

And what if Michael Jordan pointed to Jesus Christ as being the One who expanded his heart through His own lavish display of grace?

"My hope is that you won't just go down in history as being one of the greatest basketball players of all time," Jesus might say to Jordan. "While that's a terrific accomplishment and something to be proud of, I hope there's more, because whether you like it or not, you're a role model for a lot of young people.

"So I hope your legacy will be that you were a man who looked deep inside yourself and harnessed your competitiveness before it took you over the edge. I hope you're remembered as a man who drew upon the courage and peace of God to cope with the tragedy that befell your father. And I hope history records you as a man who honored the God who gifted you, and out of gratitude for that gift, you lavished your resources to ease the pain of the needy and to point people toward Me."

That's the kind of legacy that would make Jesus smile.

6

What Jesus Would Say to
Bill Clinton

In recent decades religion has added a new volatility to the already turbulent world of presidential politics.

John Kennedy had to defuse the Catholic issue before becoming the first of his faith to be elected to our highest office. Later came Jimmy Carter, who made "born again" a household term. Some fretted when charismatic Christian Pat Robertson sought the Republican nomination, although, interestingly, candidate Jesse Jackson's Baptist credentials seemed to foster few fears. Ronald Reagan was the darling of the Moral Majority, while his successor, George Bush, tried to reassure that same constituency by declaring on the eve of the 1988 election: "There was never any doubt that Jesus Christ was my Savior and Lord."

Then came Bill Clinton, and the religion controversy has been heightened to a whole new level.

Clinton's own denomination, the Southern Baptists, decried his stands on abortion and homosexual rights. Abortion foe Randall Terry said it would be "a sin against God" to vote for

Clinton. The Christian Coalition mobilized its 300,000 members to oppose him, and several nationally prominent ministers, including Jerry Falwell and D. James Kennedy, hammered him on questions of character.

"If his wife cannot rely upon him to keep his vows of fidelity to her in marriage, then why should the country be expected to believe that he would keep his vows made in the assumption of his office?" D. James Kennedy asked.

Some pundits said that next to the economy, religion turned out to be the most influential factor in deciding which way a person voted in the 1992 election. And after the balloting was over, the controversy didn't evaporate. Clinton's efforts to lift the ban on homosexuals in the military and remove impediments to abortion have fueled opposition by large numbers of Christians.

A "Genuine and Sincere" Faith

Clinton has claimed that his faith in God is a cornerstone of his life. He said he became a Christian at the age of ten, and he has been an active church participant for years. In fact, during the campaign, two former pastors of Clinton and Vice President Al Gore issued a joint statement: "Our experience with [them] over the years in worship, prayer, and in public and private conversations confirms our pastoral convictions that these are men whose heads and hearts have been baptized by divine grace and mercy. We believe their walk with God to be genuine and sincere."

Rex Horne, Clinton's longtime Baptist pastor from Arkansas, told *U.S. News & World Report:* "On the homosexual thing, I never heard him say [that allowing gays in the military] is an endorsement of a lifestyle. And he is pro-choice, not pro-abortion. He is portrayed as being further left on these issues than I believe him to be."

Clinton's "quest for spiritual fulfillment," as one magazine put it, became popular grist for the news media as his first year in office was coming to a close. Aides said the nation's spiraling crime rate had "turned the president inward." Articles described how he often prayed with his daughter, Chelsea, at bedtime and chatted with his Arkansas pastor by phone on Saturday nights.

The president has often said, as have many of his predecessors, that he looks to God for help. And so here's the question: What kind of spiritual guidance would the most powerful being in the universe provide to the most powerful individual on the planet? In fact, what would God say about the subject of leadership that would equally apply to all of us who find ourselves in a position of authority, whether it's in government, business, industry, labor, or some other arena?

As with the other people profiled in this book, I'm sure there would be a lot that Jesus would discuss with Bill Clinton. But in focusing on the topic of Clinton's leadership, I think Jesus might very well quote from Psalm 78, which closes with God elevating the shepherd David from his agrarian background to the post of king over Israel. The poem ends with this description of how he ended up governing the people: "And David shepherded them with integrity of heart; with skillful hands he led them."

I could imagine Jesus saying to the president, who rose from the largely rural state of Arkansas to the highest office of the land: "Bill, you're occupying the most difficult and influential position in the world, so you must make sure of this: that you wield your power with a heart of integrity and with hands of skill."

The Integrity Equation

Quickly, without looking it up: what's an integer? Do you remember from high school math? Okay, I'll admit it—I had to check my son's textbook. An integer, I rediscovered, is a whole number, like five or twenty or 100, as opposed to a fraction, like one-half or one-third.

So how does that mathematical concept shed light on what Jesus would mean by telling Clinton that he should lead America with a heart of integrity?

Well, author Warren Wiersbe has pointed out that *integer* and *integrity* come from the same root word. This can help us pin down what integrity really means—it suggests wholeness, completeness, or entirety. Another related word is *integrated*, which is when all aspects of your life are working together in harmony.

You see, Jesus wants us to function as *whole* people. In fact, He said in Matthew 6:24 that nobody can serve two masters at the same time. Why? Because attempting to do so would fragment our loyalties and splinter our allegiances.

So for a Christian, integrity means a wholeness or integration between your *beliefs* and *behavior*, between your *creed* and *character*, and between your *faith* and your *formulation of policies*. A person with integrity has consistency. What he believes is how he acts. What he says is what he does. His faith isn't segregated into one area of his life but is marbled throughout everything he does.

This has profound implications for Christians who are leaders, whether they're running a company or a country. For instance, a leader who's a Christian shouldn't just believe that all people matter to God, but he needs to live that out in his day-to-day dealings with people. That truth should influence the creation of his policies and shape his attitudes toward those who don't matter much in the eyes of society: AIDS victims, those crushed by poverty, victims of discrimination, and the most vulnerable of all, the unborn.

Integrity means that a leader who's a Christian doesn't just believe in the biblical value of truth-telling, but puts it into practice when deciding whether to break his promises or to keep them, whether to cover up his mistakes or come clean about them, and whether to choose deception when it will suit his purposes.

Integrity means that a leader who's a Christian doesn't just believe in justice, but he tries to demonstrate fairness and impartiality in dealing with all people—not just the politically correct, the well connected, or campaign contributors.

Integrity means that a leader who's a Christian doesn't just talk about God's compassion, but he lives out that compassion in trying to alleviate the pain of the poor by helping them in practical ways to meet their physical, medical, and other needs.

Integrity means that a leader who's a Christian doesn't just intellectually agree with the character traits that Jesus promoted—qualities like humility, servanthood, personal purity, and forgiveness—but he lives out those characteristics whether the public spotlight is on or off.

Interior Matters of the Heart

Unfortunately there's a tendency—and this is especially true of political leaders—to have a faith they consider strictly private. Bring up religion and they respond, "Well, my faith is a very personal thing. I like to keep it to myself." David Lewis Stokes, Jr., an author and rector of St. Stephen's (Episcopal) Church in Providence, Rhode Island, observed:

> I note a cultural shift. At one time religious discourse was a formative voice in our ongoing American conversation. But . . . America now seems committed to what we might call the personalization of religion. That means religious faith defined as an interior matter of the heart, a personal concern much like one's preference for a dental floss or deodorant. When belief happens to coincide with accepted public policy, why, well and good. When it stands at odds with this policy, religion is— don't y'all know?—*personal.*

I'm not saying leaders need to shout their beliefs from the rooftops or quote Bible verses all the time. *But a faith that's just an interior matter of the heart is a faith that's too small.* A person can't be taking his beliefs very seriously if he doesn't let them influence his behavior as a leader.

And this isn't just an issue for politicians. In 1993 *Newsweek* summarized three major research projects by saying: "These studies demonstrate that while religion pervades the American landscape, only a minority take it seriously." Another study by George H. Gallup concluded that only about thirteen percent of Americans have what can be considered a "transforming faith," through which their professed beliefs make a consistent day-to-day difference in their lives.

Integrity is a challenging issue for you and me. Is our faith strictly "personal"—segregated into a corner of our lives where it doesn't change the way we live? Or is there daily evidence that Jesus Christ has revolutionized our attitudes and outlook, and that this has radically changed our conduct?

So I think Jesus would say to Bill Clinton and all other leaders: "I want you to do a very courageous thing—*to lead with a heart of integrity.* That means making the tough decisions to

honor God day in and day out, even when it's not politically correct. It means letting your faith in Me shape your behavior and
your leadership, even when it costs you. It means trying, as best
you can, to lead as I would lead."

The apostle Paul put it this way in Galatians 1:10: "Am I
now trying to win the approval of men, or of God? Or am I trying
to please men? If I were still trying to please men, I would not be
a servant of Christ."

The modern equivalent would be to say, "In the end, which
constituency am I serving—people or God?" Because, as Jesus
said, ultimately a person with integrity can't simultaneously serve
two masters. Sooner or later, when push comes to shove, a choice
has to be made: Is it God or ambition that's ruling our lives?

The Importance of Discernment

In keeping with Psalm 78, Jesus might very well add: "And,
Bill, in addition to having a heart of integrity, it's critically important that you lead with hands of skill."

This phrase refers primarily to the skill of discernment,
which *Webster's* calls "an acuteness of judgment and understanding." In fact, that's what another leader, King Solomon, requested
when he said to God in 1 Kings 3:9: "So give your servant a discerning heart to govern your people and to distinguish between
right and wrong." A few verses later, God rewarded Solomon for
his unselfish request, saying, "I will do what you have asked. I will
give you a wise and discerning heart" (v. 12).

Discernment is one of the most important skills a leader
can possess. For instance, this kind of sensitive judgment is
needed in order to determine when it's legitimate to compromise
and when it's imperative to stand firm.

We know that there are always going to be pressures to
compromise in life, especially in politics. For instance, early in his
presidency, Clinton was trying to have some key legislation
passed. In order to ensure votes from certain congressmen, he
had to tinker with the farm support system, military base closings,
peanut imports, honeybee subsidies—and he even had to promise
to play golf with one representative!

Like it or not, that's how American politics are played. And if you're a leader in any kind of enterprise, then you know that you end up playing certain games, too. But the discerning leader knows how to play the game without violating God's rules. He knows when to stop before a compromise would impinge on his soul by eroding a core value or violating a biblical belief.

For example, it's customary for politicians and business leaders to try to put a positive spin on a negative event. Some consultants are nicknamed "spin doctors" because their role is to try to influence the media by putting an incident in the best possible light for their client.

That's okay up to a point. But a discerning leader knows when to step in and say, "Wait a minute—it's fine to look at something from a positive perspective and emphasize the good side, but now we're starting to go beyond that. We're starting to distort and mislead and lie—and *that's* where I draw the line."

Christians who are business leaders face a similar challenge. When does "wining and dining" a customer slip over the line into becoming improper influence? At what point in the selling process does emphasizing a product's positive attributes become a distortion? When does a legitimate critique of a competitor become unfair gossip and slander?

It takes discernment and courage for any leader to create God-honoring boundaries and then to stick to them despite the temptation to win at any cost.

The Bible in a Pluralistic Culture

Discernment is also needed to understand how to govern in a pluralistic society. After all, the United States is not a theocracy. We're not ruled directly by the Bible but by a Constitution, which in turn is rooted in Judeo-Christian values. People are allowed to believe in whatever faith they desire.

So while there are overarching moral truths from God that apply in all societies—for instance, the sanctity of human life, before and after birth—some behaviors that the Bible calls sin probably can't be effectively outlawed in a secular and pluralistic culture where many belief systems are allowed.

For instance, using God's name as a swear word is clearly against God's law, but do we want to ban expletives in a society which allows religious diversity? Extramarital affairs are quite properly called sinful by the Bible, but should we pass laws to throw people in jail for cheating on their spouse? And what about private, consensual homosexual behavior? The Bible clearly calls it a sin, but should we be investigating and prosecuting people for engaging in that kind of conduct? Careful discernment is needed to determine where appropriate lines should be drawn.

Sometimes unbiblical behavior may have to be permitted under secular law, but a discerning leader will realize when he should use the moral force of his office to try to convince people that they should make the choice to follow God's path anyway. After all, just because something is legal doesn't mean it's right or moral or desirable—or that our society should endorse it, promote it, encourage it, or give it any special privileges. There are times when a Christian leader needs to stand up and say, "I feel a responsibility to tell you clearly and forcefully where I stand on this moral issue."

One of Clinton's biggest lessons of his first year in office, he told *U.S. News & World Report*, was that he could effectively shape the national debate on spiritual matters: "I think I underestimated the importance of the President's voice, just being able to speak about these issues in a coherent, clear, and forceful way."

Yet so far Clinton has failed to do that in the abortion arena. He believes that in our pluralistic society abortion should be made available so women can decide individually whether to pursue that alternative to pregnancy. His position is that abortion should be "safe, legal—and rare."

However, abortion is anything *but* rare! There are 1.5 *million* abortions a year in the United States. Even so, I've never heard Clinton speak out with passion and conviction to urge women to choose life for their baby. He hasn't used the considerable power of the president's voice to take a personal moral stand that would attempt to dissuade women from abortion and to persuade them to pursue adoption instead. As a result, the message people are getting isn't that he merely *tolerates* abortion, but that he *endorses* it.

A discerning leader wrestles with the matter of how far Christians can go in incorporating biblical standards into secular law. Many times these matters are very difficult to pin down. But he also knows he has a responsibility as a Christ-follower to speak out in expressing his beliefs as a way of providing moral guidance to his constituents.

The Collision of Values

In addition, discernment is needed to figure out which course to pursue when competing moral values clash. And in Washington, D.C.—as well as in every statehouse and city hall and school district in America —values are colliding all the time. Listen to the perspective of political veteran Dan Coats, a Christian who is a U.S. senator from Indiana:

> How do you make a decision between a better environment and the jobs it will cost? The dignity of employment and our stewardship over creation both demand moral attention. Is a cleaner river worth regulations that eliminate 30 jobs, 300 jobs, 3,000 jobs? How do you weigh cleaner air against the broken spirit of the unemployed?
>
> How do you choose between fighting poverty and fighting dependency? How do you pursue generous compassion when it risks the slow destruction of the spirit we see in generation after generation of a welfare underclass?
>
> How do you choose between a reverence for life and the use of fetal tissue from abortions to treat the victims of Parkinson's disease? How do you provide hope to those who suffer, when it risks covering the horror of abortion with a veneer of scientific progress and public service?

These are the kind of tough calls that our leaders are facing with increasing frequency. Standing alone, Christianity's moral standards are crystal clear. "But some of the greatest agony I have known as a member of Congress has come when those clear, commanding moral precepts collide," Coats said in a speech. "Sometimes every option is tainted by suffering and sin. Sometimes each alternative is made uncomfortable by a hybrid of good and evil.

Sometimes we are left with the murky battle between bad and worse."

That's the reason we not only need integrity among our leaders, but also godly discernment. And that's why I think Jesus would say to the president: "Bill, you can't take the easy way out. You must lead with skillful hands."

Of course, Clinton's response—and yours, for that matter—might very well be, "Okay, but how do I *do* that? I'm going to need some help if I'm going to pull that off."

One important step can be found in another statement that Jesus might very well make to Bill Clinton: "Whatever you do, listen to My voice above the clamor of the crowds."

Drowning Out the Truth

Everybody knows that lobbyists and crowds are always trying to influence what politicians do, and that's a legitimate part of the governing process. But the Bible describes an ugly incident that demonstrates what can happen when a politician listens to them to the exclusion of God.

The story involves the trial of Jesus before Pontius Pilate, the governor of Judea. Pilate knew Jesus was innocent; in fact, he admitted it three times. So where did Pilate go wrong?

Well, Pilate listened to lobbyists from the religious establishment who whispered in his ear that they wanted this trouble-maker put to death. This special interest group was very powerful, as is often the case. Pilate had already tangled with them on a previous issue and suffered an embarrassing political setback, and he didn't want to risk getting on their wrong side again. So when they spoke, he listened.

Then Pilate turned to the crowd because, hey, you've got to let the people speak, right? He asked whether they wanted him to free a criminal named Barabbas or the innocent Jesus. For their own reasons, the crowd responded: "Free Barabbas!"

The lobbyists spoke, the crowd spoke—and Jesus spoke, too. He told Pilate in John 18:37: "Everyone on the side of truth listens to me."

But Pilate responded with the cynicism of a political hack. "What," he asked, "is truth?"

Remember what Pilate did after that? He washed his hands of the whole matter, as if to symbolically say, "Well, I'm personally opposed to killing innocent people, but that's just my private belief. So I'll do whatever the people want." Doesn't that sound a lot like modern politicians who say they have a personal conviction about something, but that it's just an interior matter of the heart? They don't let it affect their leadership or public policies, and so they allow themselves to merely go along with whatever the polls say is popular.

Do you see what has happened? Pilate let the whining of lobbyists and the roaring of the crowd drown out the voice of truth that was coming from Jesus.

And Jesus might very well say to Bill Clinton today, "Don't be swayed by political insiders or by the shifting opinions of the populace to do anything that contradicts what I've told you is right. My truth doesn't change. Above the clamor of the crowd, be attuned to My voice."

The Value of Advisers

How do we become attuned to Jesus' voice? Not by just being a churchgoer, but by nurturing a flourishing, authentic, day-to-day relationship with God. Not by merely reading and quoting the Bible, but by letting biblical truth reshape our view of the world. We do it by asking God for His wisdom, which the Bible says in James 1:5 that He's generous in providing.

And we do it by having godly advisers who can help us grapple with the interface of spiritual truth and everyday life. After all, a president has media advisers, political advisers, foreign affairs advisers, military advisers, economic advisers, image advisers—even his advisers have advisers. Shouldn't he also have some spiritual counselors who could give ongoing input on how to govern with a heart of integrity and with hands of skill? Proverbs 11:14 says, "For lack of guidance, a nation falls, but many advisers make victory sure."

Many advisers; that's important. As I was researching Clinton's life, I discovered that when he went to his pastor years ago to hash out what his position on abortion should be, this particular minister said that, in his interpretation of Scripture, life doesn't begin until a baby takes his first breath. That now-deceased minister played a pivotal role in shaping Clinton's view on the subject of abortion.

I think Clinton did the right thing by seeking counsel, but this pastor's viewpoint flies in the face of the prevailing scholarly understanding of what the Bible teaches. That's an example of why it's important to have many godly advisers so that, in the end, balanced advice can be provided.

It was encouraging during Clinton's first year in office that he scheduled a few meetings with Christian leaders for informal discussions at the White House. In light of vociferous Christian opposition to Clinton, these leaders showed courage for being willing to meet with him. But what's really needed is a core of trusted advisers who can provide biblical insights and spiritual wisdom on a consistent basis and who feel the freedom to challenge or cheer the president on any matter, foreign or domestic.

And it isn't just the president who needs a spiritual board of directors. Every Christian does.

Often after I speak at a church, people ask my advice concerning an important issue or decision in their lives. Sometimes I'll say, "I don't really know you and all of your circumstances. Do you have some godly men or women who you share your life with and who can give you some biblical counsel for your specific situation?" Unfortunately most respond with a blank stare.

Think about it: *If you were faced with a crossroads of the heart, who would you go to for advice on which path to take?*

If nobody's name pops into your mind, why not take the initiative to develop a small group of Christians with whom you can meet on a regular basis for discussions of life issues, prayer, encouragement, and accountability?

As for me, I don't know what I'd do without the close friends I meet with twice a month for spiritual input and frank discussions about our lives. They know enough about me so that when I need practical insights on which way to turn, they're prepared to provide thoughtful and godly wisdom to keep me on track. "As iron sharpens iron," says Proverbs 27:17, "so one man sharpens another."

"That's What I Want to Be"

The day after Christmas, less than a month before he was sworn into office, Bill Clinton attended a gathering of ministers in Little Rock. At the end of the evening, one of the preachers handed him a plaque. Engraved were the words of Psalm 78:72: "And David shepherded them with integrity of heart; with skillful hands he led them."

According to one report, Clinton was visibly moved by the gesture. "That's what I want to be," said the president-elect.

As we've seen, the words from that psalm—"integrity of heart" and "skillful hands"—are brimming with meaning. How well Clinton abides by their teaching will determine how God—and how history—will judge his leadership.

I want to end with one other thing that I could very well imagine Jesus saying to the president. "Bill," He might say, "it's important for you to know this: I've asked My people to pray for you—and many of them have been doing so."

The Bible tells all Christians in Romans 13 to honor and submit to the civil authorities who govern them. The apostle Peter, during the reign of the merciless Roman Emperor Nero, wrote in 1 Peter 2:17: "Show proper respect to everyone: Love the brotherhood of believers, fear God, honor the king." And 1 Timothy 2:1–2 says: "I urge, then, first of all, that requests, prayers, intercession and thanksgiving be made for everyone—for kings and all those in authority."

I know lots of Christians who are complying with those verses in the case of Bill Clinton. They're praying for him and for the future of our country.

But I've also run into many Christians who are blatantly ignoring these biblical injunctions. There has been gloating over some of Clinton's problems, as well as a lot of self-righteousness and name-calling. And there are Christian organizations that have been raising funds by unfairly painting everything Clinton does in the worst possible light and triumphantly recounting his failures. Yet the Bible says in Proverbs 24:17: "Do not gloat when your enemy falls; when he stumbles, do not let your heart rejoice."

I was having lunch one day with a nationally prominent Republican. Since I was mulling over this topic, I asked, "What do you think Jesus would say to Bill Clinton?" Well, he really unloaded. He told me a couple of cynical jokes about Clinton and his wife that were going around Washington, and then he took a few below-the-belt shots at him.

But then there was a pause. I think he may have been feeling a little embarrassed. A few moments later, he said softly: "Well, I suppose Jesus would say something to me, too. I think He'd tell me, 'You who are without sin, cast the first stone.'"

I thought, *"That's* the kind of humble attitude we need to foster."

"I Did Not Vote for You"

One thing that distinguishes authentic Christians from others is that they don't just love the people they agree with, but they also love those who they *disagree* with.

After all, there's nothing wrong with disagreeing with our leaders; in fact, Christians have a responsibility to actively oppose legislation and government initiatives they don't believe are in the country's best interests. Christians are free to vigorously critique Clinton and to consider character issues when deciding whether to support him politically. Certainly there are areas where I strongly disagree with him, especially in some of the key appointments he has made. But the *way* all of this is done matters to God.

In a newsletter called *Discernment,* Christian author Bob Moeller wrote:

> Those who consider themselves political and moral conservatives have a unique opportunity at this point in our nation's history. One option is to play hardball politics and rejoice as their opponents stumble; the other is to display love and mercy in the midst of a highly polarized and angry culture. Is it possible to show gentleness and compassion to a person we might disagree with on so many issues? That's both the challenge and the opportunity. The President thinks he understands the mind of a moral and spiritual conservative. He believes it's filled with hostility, anger, and a desire for power. What are we doing to change his mind?

What about it? What am I doing? And what are *you* doing?

Near the end of Clinton's first year in office, he invited a group of Christian leaders to the White House, and each participant was given an opportunity to talk to Clinton about whatever was on his mind. Writer Mike Yaconelli reported the words of one pastor that impressed me as being a sensitive and Christlike approach:

"Mr. President, I did not vote for you," the minister began. "When I awakened the morning after the election, I was somewhat shaken that you had won. My first reaction was one of alarm and concern. Almost immediately God began to speak to me. For the next few hours I prayed about what my response should be to your election. The next Sunday, I stood in my pulpit and told the congregation, 'William Clinton is our new President, and it is our responsibility to pray for him and to love him.' Mr. President, I want to tell you that I love you and am praying for you."

That, I believe, is a godly attitude. Yet in our highly charged political atmosphere, even praying for the president can be controversial. For instance, when word got out that Billy Graham had been asked to offer a prayer at Clinton's inaugural, Graham was inundated with letters urging him to say no. Christian organizations tried to dissuade him from publicly praying for the nation's new leader, suggesting that this might be misconstrued as an endorsement of all his policies. Though they were pursuing different agendas, both liberals and conservatives finally seemed to be united on one thing: They didn't want Graham praying at the inaugural. That's *amazing* to me!

But Graham did pray. And to end this chapter on what Jesus might say to our president, I want to offer the same prayer that Graham presented on the day that Bill Clinton and Al Gore took office. I'm doing so because these sentiments are also the prayer of my heart—and I hope of yours as well.

> Our God and Our Father, we thank You for the moral and spiritual foundations which our forefathers gave us, and which are rooted deeply in Holy Scripture. Those principles have nourished and guided us as a nation in the past.
>
> But we cannot say that we are a righteous people, for we are not. We have sinned against You. We have sown to the wind and are now reaping the whirlwind of crime,

drug abuse, racism, immorality, and social injustice. We need to repent of our sins and turn by faith to You.

And now we commit to You President Clinton and Vice President Gore, whom You have permitted to take leadership at this critical time in our nation's history. Help them always to see the office to which they have been elected as a sacred trust from You. We pray that You will bless their wives, who will share so much of the responsibility and burdens.

May President Clinton know that he is never really alone, but that the eternal God can be his refuge, and that he can turn to You in every circumstance. Give him the wisdom You have promised to those who ask, and the strength that You alone can give.

I pray this in the name of the One who was called "Wonderful Counselor, the mighty God, the everlasting Father, the Prince of Peace."

Amen.

7

What Jesus Would Say to
Donald Trump

Two scenes, separated by fourteen years and a mountain of money.

Scene One:

Most people looked at the dilapidated Commodore Hotel on Manhattan's East Forty-second Street and saw a dingy eyesore in a rapidly deteriorating neighborhood.

Donald John Trump, just thirty years old and not long out of the Wharton School, stood alone in front of the run-down structure and gazed up at it.

He saw the seeds of success.

The fast-talking Trump offered $10 million to the hotel's bankrupt owner. Then he convinced banks to loan him $80 million, the city to give him $120 million in tax abatements, and Hyatt Hotels to manage the property in return for half interest.

The process began in 1976. By 1980 the building was reopened as the sparkling Grand Hyatt Hotel, a property so successful that it revitalized the whole area—and stuffed a $15 million-a-year profit into young Trump's pocket.

From that start, Trump, the son of a well-to-do housing developer, parlayed deal after deal into a financial empire once estimated to be worth $1.7 billion. By 1989 *Forbes* magazine listed him as the nineteenth wealthiest American. Everything he touched, it seemed, glittered like gold.

In New York there was the $200 million Trump Tower; the thirty-seven-story Trump Plaza; and Trump Parc, overlooking Central Park. In Atlantic City, there was the Trump Taj Mahal (triple the size of its Indian namesake), Trump Plaza, Trump Regency, and Trump Castle. In Florida, there was Trump Plaza of the Palm Beaches and the 118-room Mar-a-Lago hideaway. In the air was the *Trump Shuttle*; in the water was the $29 million *Trump Princess* yacht; on the ground was the Trump Cadillac. And in bookstores was the runaway best-seller, *Trump: The Art of the Deal*.

His moniker was plastered on so many upscale projects that *Doonesbury* ran a parody in which a giddy Trump decided to change his name. "Trump T. Trump!" he declared. "I like it! It screams quality!"

An Empire of Sand

Scene Two:

The year was 1990, and Donald Trump was walking with his girlfriend in front of Tiffany's jewelers in New York City. He pointed to a blind man with a tin cup and a mangy dog. "How would you like to know he is worth $900 million more than me today?" Trump asked.

He wasn't joking. The beggar may have had a net worth of zero, but Trump was nearly a *billion* dollars in the hole.

Trump's plummet from the financial Mount Everest into the Death Valley of debt was one of the most dramatic reverses of the decade. His airline had to be sold. So did his yacht and his personal Boeing 727. He forfeited half of his largest casino. Some of his properties sought bankruptcy protection. And he lost his wife, Ivana, in a messy—and expensive—divorce.

Comedians relentlessly poked fun at him. Quipped Jay Leno: "Ivana's on vacation in Italy. She threw a coin in a fountain. Donald jumped in after it!" And Number Five on David Letterman's *Top Ten Things Overheard on Earth Day* was: "That's right—you get a nickel for every can, Mr. Trump!"

Chirped the *New York Post:* "Uh-Owe!" Gloated *Newsweek*: "Trump: The Fall." Everybody, it seemed, relished reading about his fast-fading fortunes. In German, it's a phenomenon called *schadenfreude*—delighting over the humiliation of the high and mighty.

The often boastful Trump, once a media darling thanks to his manipulation of reporters, was on the verge of losing it all. His reputation as a straight-shooter was tarnished through tell-all books written by alienated business associates and journalists who described him as deceitful, temperamental, and hypocritical. His popularity among working-class America—he was once nicknamed "The People's Billionaire"—was jeopardized by disclosures of his marital infidelity.

And his financial empire was teetering because of his practice of mortgaging his properties to the hilt, which worked fine until a stalled economy strangled his cash flow. That meant he had difficulty making his gargantuan payments, and glum-faced bankers and bondholders came knocking. Chastened by the savings and loan scandals, they weren't in the mood to extend more credit.

He was definitely down—but not out. At least, not yet.

King of the Comeback?

"I'm back!"

Though one business publication scoffed that it was "a massive display of wishful thinking," Donald was trumpeting to the world in 1993 that he was finally on the road to recovery.

As the year closed, he had managed to whittle his personal debt down to about $115 million. In a dazzling ceremony, he married his longtime girlfriend, who was photographed wearing a $2 million diamond tiara.

And the incurable deal-weaver was busy from Tokyo to Las Vegas to Gulfport, Mississippi, trying to pull off projects that would open his cash spigot once again. His latest undertaking: another book, this one optimistically titled *Trump: The Comeback.* "Should Trump be counted out?" asked *Business Week.* "Not entirely."

Unbowed by his ordeal, Trump declared, "I've learned that I'm the toughest _____ around."

Whatever happens to Trump, his name has become synonymous with success—his quest for it, his achievement of it, his loss of it, and his renewed campaign to recapture it against great odds. "Like J. P. Morgan or John D. Rockefeller, Trump has transformed his name into a symbol of success—a myth that transcends the rockier reality," wrote journalist Mary Beth Sheridan.

In fact, I've talked to many people who have only a vague recollection of Trump's financial free-fall. They still associate his name with accomplishment and prosperity. And, to be sure, Trump's not on public assistance. One banker was quoted as saying, "He's got maybe $1 million in cash, and that's it"—as if that were small change!

So I think of all the issues Jesus might discuss with Trump—and there would undoubtedly be a litany of them—He might very well touch on the topic of success. After all, Jesus knows that dangers lurk in the shadows on the road to riches. Just as He cautioned the wealthy of His day, I believe He would lovingly counsel anyone who's on the fast track of achievement in the 1990s.

The Illusion of Success

Somehow I can't picture Jesus sitting in the overstuffed armchair across from Trump's elegant gull-wing Brazilian rosewood desk in his opulent office at The Trump Organization's headquarters. Instead, maybe Jesus would take him for a walk in Central Park, where He might say, "Donald, let me give you a bit of advice: It's critically important that you learn how to guard against the illusion of success."

You see, the illusion of success is thinking we're succeeding in life, but the reality is that we're measuring success by a gauge that isn't telling us the whole story.

For instance, the way our society has traditionally kept score on who's successful and who isn't is by how much money they've accumulated. That's how Trump has referred to money— as life's scorekeeper. And so people strive to build an impressive investment portfolio, and when they do, they say to themselves, "This must be what success in life feels like."

Since I'm a pastor, you're probably expecting me to declare at this point: "But money won't buy happiness!" Or, "Money will never bring you any satisfaction!" But I'm not going to do that because those statements are not true.

The reality of the matter is this: Money *can* buy some happiness, bring some fulfillment, buy a certain amount of freedom. Money *can* make life more comfortable. As one well-known entertainer once said, "I've been rich and I've been poor, and being rich is better!"

But author Warren Wiersbe made a very astute observation in his book *The Integrity Crisis*. "The problem is not that money *doesn't* satisfy, but that it *does*," he wrote. "However, it satisfies only those people who are willing to live on a low level where money brings them their greatest happiness."

In other words the illusion of success is that you think you're being successful when you're making fistfuls of money, even though the reality is that you might be settling for too little. You're setting your sights too low. You're cheating yourself out of a deeper and more meaningful kind of fulfillment. You think, *This must be what success feels like*, when in actuality you're experiencing just a shadow of what ultimate success really is.

In fact, a researcher recently conducted a study of 4,126 executives and professional people who were considered successful by economic standards. Yet a majority of them—six out of ten—said that even though they were financially satisfied, their lives felt empty and meaningless.

They were under the illusion that they were successful because society's measuring gauge told them they were, but they had a nagging feeling that *real* success must involve something more.

And it does.

A Craving for Community

God created us with a gnawing hunger to be in loving community with Him, and so it makes sense that the ultimate success in life is for us to have that relational hunger satisfied. It's like the song we sometimes sing at our church: "He satisfies my soul." *That's* the gauge for measuring real success—is your soul *being* satisfied?

So shoot straight with me: *Is it, really?* Does your life have a richness of meaning and purpose? Honestly—does it?

Do you feel secure and loved and accepted by God? Are you feeling more and more like you really do matter to Him?

Is your relationship with Him fulfilling and flourishing? Be candid—are you growing in that area?

Are you experiencing the exhilaration of living life as a daring adventure out on the edge of faith? Are you taking steps to trust God more and more with your daily circumstances?

Is your sense of community with your family and friends becoming deeper and more authentic over time? The question isn't whether you have associates or partners or buddies—the issue is whether your soul is knit to other human beings.

If your city were hit by an earthquake tomorrow, and you were to lose every possession you had—*how rich would you still be?* I like the comment by one survivor of California's devastating 1994 earthquake, who pointed to the rubble of his house and said, "I've come to realize that's just stuff over there. I'm here, I'm alive, and the *real stuff* is God."

I guess I'm asking: How rich are you in the *real stuff* of God? In other words, *is your soul being satisfied?*

I think Jesus would challenge every person who's on a financial fast-track by saying: "Don't settle for the illusion of success. Don't be content with the kind of surface-level fulfillment that your purchasing power can buy. Because if you are, you're cheating yourself out of something much more rewarding. Money's okay; it has its place. But the problem with money is that it just isn't the currency that can buy soul satisfaction—and that's what you've been created to crave."

Gaining the World

For some, the measuring gauge of success isn't money but some other form of achievement. For example, I remember when my life revolved around my accomplishments as a journalist. I pursued my career to the exclusion of my wife, my children, and God. And I had enough awards and front-page bylines to prove that I was a success in the eyes of my peers.

Then one day while working at the *Chicago Tribune*, I went down to the library where they keep clippings of articles. I needed to look at a particular story I had written about a year earlier, so the librarian took me over to a huge filing cabinet.

"We take one copy of every article," she explained, "and we file it away under the name of the reporter who wrote it." She pulled out a broad, shallow file drawer, and inside were rows packed with yellow envelopes that were stamped *Lee Strobel*. "Here you go," she said. "These are all your articles."

I had a strange sensation as I stared at that drawer. Here was the substance of my entire life's work at the *Tribune*. Suddenly, it struck me: *This is what I'm killing myself for?* I'm trading my life for a drawer full of neatly folded newspaper clippings that are turning brittle and yellowing around the edges? At that moment, it didn't seem like a fair trade. In fact, I was getting ripped off!

Some people trade their entire life for a drawer full of shopping receipts, or a wall full of plaques, or a bedpost full of notches, or a bankbook full of numbers. Is it really a fair trade?

What's really important in life probably will get sorted out during our last moments on earth. My guess is that many will look back and ask, "Did I accumulate a lot of stuff that I can't take with me, or did I lay up treasures for myself in heaven? Did I take time to develop a relationship with God that will last forever? Did I leave a mark on people that's going to fade, or did I leave a mark that's eternal? Did I spend my life building things that will corrode or erode over time, or did I invest in the lives of individuals who will endure into eternity? When God nudged me to take a spiritual risk, did I trust Him or play it safe?"

Jesus put it this way in Luke 9:25: "What good is it for a man to gain the whole world, and yet lose or forfeit his very self?"

And He might say to Donald Trump, "You know what it's like to gain the whole world, and now you know what it's like to lose almost everything. You've seen how precarious wealth can be. Don't keep falling for the myth that that's all success is about. Keep going deeper —with Me and with others—because the real test of success is this: *Is your soul being satisfied?"*

Escaping the Snare of Success

I think Jesus might very well say to Donald Trump and other success-oriented people: "It's also critical that you take steps to guard against the snare of success."

You see, experts like John R. O'Neil, author of *The Paradox of Success*, have noticed a trend among people who pursue success with the same laser-beam intensity that high achievers like Donald Trump do. What often happens is that while they're on the achievement track, they're unwittingly building a trap for themselves at the same time. In the end that snare can spring shut and destroy them.

How's the trap built? Let me walk you through a common scenario. As I've read about the events leading up to Trump's professional and personal meltdown, I can see evidence of virtually every one of these danger signs. So as I enumerate each point, ask yourself honestly: "Could he be talking about me, too?"

First, people with a single-minded focus on their careers slowly begin to freeze out their spouse and kids. Much of the time, they're at the office, where coworkers become a kind of surrogate family. And when they're at home, they're not *really* at home, if you know what I mean. Their minds are preoccupied, and they're often on the phone with business. As a result, their relationship with their family begins to deteriorate, and that critically important support system flickers and then is lost from their life.

Then, over time, their social circle begins to shrivel. They get wrapped up with clients, colleagues, and other people who have a vested interest in their relationship. So they gradually abandon the friends who really care about them as people apart from their careers, and that crucial support system disappears, too.

They begin working more and more hours under more and more pressure and spending less and less time recuperating. They drop the membership at the health club because they never seem to make it over there. Even if they go fishing, golfing, or to a party, it's to entertain clients or important contacts, and as a result it's not much of an escape. Consequently they never really get rejuvenated or replenished, and their health starts to slide.

And they stop taking time for solitude or introspection about their life. They feel like their time could be put to much more productive use by working. So they lose touch with themselves and their emotions, and they don't deal constructively with the dark side of their personality that may really be driving their ambition.

Then once they reach a certain level of success, they want to maintain their image at all costs, and therefore they slowly squeeze out the people who give them frank and honest feedback. These people are replaced by ambitious assistants who tell them only what they want to hear. Besides, success-driven people figure they know more about their business than anybody else. Thus they lose valuable feedback and accountability, and they become dangerously vulnerable to problems hiding in their blind spots.

After a while they stop stretching themselves in new areas of life because they want to stick with what has made them successful and what has worked in the past. Their horizons begin to shrink. Despite their success, they get increasingly bored with their stale lives. Some remain frustratingly stuck at this point, while others turn to thrill-seeking and risk-taking, including the pursuit of extramarital affairs.

Of course, God gets displaced from their life, too. Who's got time to pray or read the Bible, or meet with a small group, or seek God's guidance? If they had a relationship with God, it atrophies, and after a while they figure, "What's the big deal about God anyway? It seems like I get along fine without Him."

Pursuing God's Game Plan

Do you see the snare they're building for themselves?

They're increasingly isolated from loving and supportive relationships, out of touch with themselves, flying solo without God, making up their own rules, shut off from honest input, falling into a rut or seeking thrills through risk-taking, and they have an inflated opinion of their own abilities. It's only a matter of time before a snare like that will snap shut with devastating results.

All of us are vulnerable to this kind of trap unless we purposefully pursue success according to a game plan that keeps our lives in perspective and balance. The Bible's game plan describes how to make God the center of our life, and then how to let Him help us build family relationships and meaningful friendships, as well as maintain a balance of introspection, rejuvenation, and accountability.

Because here's the thing: If you don't intentionally set out to build your life around a God-honoring game plan, you'll probably construct a trap for yourself by default. It's too easy for us to get swayed by a culture that's chronically out of balance. Consider what well-known management consultants Tom Peters and Nancy Austin wrote a few years ago:

> The cost of excellence is the giving up of family vacations, Little League games, birthday dinners, evenings, weekends, lunch hours, gardening, reading, movies, and most other pastimes. We have a number of friends whose marriages and partnerships crumbled under the weight of their devotion to a dream. We are frequently asked if it is possible to "have it all"—a fully satisfying personal life and a fully satisfying hard working one. Our answer is no.

Friends, a success that sacrifices our family and our physical and emotional well-being is a snare that's poised to spring shut and destroy us.

And I think Jesus would tell Donald Trump and everyone else on the success track: "For your own sake, make the hard choice to follow My game plan. I designed you; it makes sense that I'd know what's best for you. My game plan works when you put Me first, your family second, and you keep your life in balance as you pursue excellence and success. And you know I'm always here to coach you through."

Love as a Business Strategy

The third caution that Jesus would offer to Trump and other financial overachievers might be this: "Whatever you do, guard against the cynicism of success."

Trump has described himself as a cynic in a rough-and-tumble business. "I'm the most vicious person," he said. "When you have an enemy, you gotta [destroy] them and devote your whole life to [destroying] them." In one case he likened himself to "a nuclear bomb waiting to drop" on a rival.

Though Trump contends that he's "very fair" toward his employees and that few people leave his employment, some former associates have called him petulant, abusive, vindictive, and intimidating, sometimes keeping ten law firms busy to make good his threats of litigation against various people.

"People who have dealt very closely with Trump have seen him show bad character and complete lack of character," said an in-depth profile in *New York* magazine. "Exposing his children, fighting Ivana, insulting and suing the defenseless, tormenting his executives is the other side of the Trump charm."

All too often, successful people can become corroded with arrogance and pride. They develop a sense of superiority that convinces them that employees are tools, not people; that rules were made for others, not themselves; and that the end always justifies the means, however unsavory that may be. For some, ethics become mere abstract topics for pointy-head academics who don't understand the real world.

A while ago I came across some promotional literature for a book aimed at corporate executives. "In Chapter Two, we will show you how to cheat your employees first, before they cheat you," the material said, although I'm using "cheat" as a substitute for the obscene word that was actually used. "How to keep them smiling on low pay, how to maneuver them into low-paying jobs they are afraid to walk away from, how to fire them so you always make money." Unfortunately that's the attitude of a lot of people in business.

But it doesn't have to be that way. Jesus told His followers in Matthew 10:16: "Be as shrewd as snakes and as innocent as doves." In modern parlance that means a Christian business executive can be astute and aggressive, competitive and results-oriented, but still retain a godly character of humility, servant-hood, and genuine concern for others—including employees and competitors.

I once talked to a business leader who had recently retired from a tremendously successful career as vice president of one of the country's biggest corporations. He had been responsible for a division with more than 7,500 employees, and he was hailed from coast to coast as an outstanding executive who achieved stunning results.

"What made you such an effective leader?" I asked. He paused for a moment, then said, "Well, I just took principles from the Bible and put them into action on the job." His big discovery, he said, was this: "*Love is a legitimate business strategy.*" He proved it by the way he treated his employees and customers; they flourished, and so did he.

How about you? How do you treat the people you work with? Do you look them in the eye and call them by name, or is it, "Hey, you?" Do you see them merely as vehicles for your own advancement, or do you treat them with respect and dignity as people created in God's image? Do you ever sit down with them on their turf with no agenda of your own, just to talk? Do you ever catch them doing something right and let them know you've noticed?

In other words have you found out firsthand how love can be a legitimate business strategy?

Winning Through Integrity

Today progressive businesses are rediscovering the impor-tance of leading with a servant's attitude, treating employees with dignity, and maintaining high ethical standards. Books like *The Power of Ethical Management* and *Winning Through Integrity* have gained wide readership. Business schools are adding ethics courses, and more than 90 percent of the Fortune 500 companies now require their employees to subscribe to an ethics code.

"No society anywhere will compete very long or success-fully with people stabbing each other in the back; with people try-ing to steal from each other; with everything requiring notarized confirmation because you can't trust the other fellow; with every little squabble ending in litigation," the chairman of one of America's biggest companies said in a speech. "That is a recipe not only for headaches in running a company; it is a recipe for a nation to become wasteful, inefficient, and noncompetitive. There is no escaping this fact: the greater the measure of mutual trust and confidence in the ethics of a society, the greater its economic strength."

The bottom line is this: Ethics and management principles drawn from biblical concepts are good for business. And you don't have to be a major corporation to find that out.

I was talking with someone from our church who owns a medium-sized firm that he operates according to biblical ethics. Even though he has lost out on getting a few customers because they wanted him to breach ethical boundaries, his business has succeeded in the long run because he built a reputation as a businessman who can be trusted and as an employer who treats his workers as people who matter to God.

And he has discovered the personal benefits of God-centered management. When we do business with Christian integrity, we don't have to spend our time fretting that someone is going to uncover our lies. We don't have to endure an ongoing, low-level sense of anxiety about getting caught by government regulators. We don't have to stockpile excuses and dream up rationalizations. We can mail our tax returns on April 15 and sleep well that night.

One of my close friends, Russ Robinson, is the senior partner of a law firm that's dedicated to biblical principles. "One of the greatest benefits has been the ability to be forgetful," he told me. "In other words I don't have to struggle to remember when I've told the truth and when I've lied. I don't have to expend a lot of energy trying to keep my stories straight."

That gives a tremendous sense of freedom—to be relieved of having to mentally track a bunch of excuses and deceptions; to take pride in decisions instead of being pestered by regrets; to have a healthy sense of self-respect and a reputation that engenders trust from others.

Jesus would encourage everyone to guard against the cynicism that can corrode the way they do business. In fact, maybe

He'd quote Proverbs 10:9: "The man of integrity walks securely, but he who takes crooked paths will be found out."

God Has Emotions, Too

After sensitizing him to the illusion of success, the trap of success, and the cynicism of success, I believe Jesus might add one other caution to Donald Trump and all millionaire wannabes: "Guard against the amnesia of success."

Success can pump up people with so much self-congratulation over their accomplishments that they forget it was God Himself who gave them the ability to excel in the first place. Asked at the height of his financial success who should get the credit for his accomplishments, Trump replied: "I worked hard and didn't inherit what I've built. Hey, I made it myself."

This tendency isn't new. The Bible says in Deuteronomy 8:12–14, "When you eat and are satisfied, when you build fine houses and settle down, and when your herds and flocks grow large and your silver and gold increase and all you have is multiplied, then your heart will become proud and you will forget the LORD your God."

It's like the story about a newspaper reporter who decided to write an article about a local millionaire famous for having pulled himself up by his own bootstraps. "Tell me the story of your success," the reporter said.

The millionaire replied with obvious pride: "When I got married, my wife and I only had one nickel between us. Just five cents! But that didn't deter me. No, sir! I used that nickel to buy a crummy looking apple, and then I spent the whole evening polishing it to a brilliant shine. The next day I sold it for ten cents. I used that to buy two more apples, and I spent the evening polishing them until they were gorgeous, and then I sold them for twenty cents. And so it went, day after day, until I had finally managed to accumulate $1.60."

"Wow! This is really inspiring!" said the reporter. "What an example of a self-made man! Then what happened?"

The millionaire paused. "Well," he said with some reluctance, "the next day my father-in-law died and left us twenty million dollars."

It's human nature to want to talk more about the part we played in our success than to acknowledge God's much greater role.

But the Bible cautions us a little further along in that same passage from Deuteronomy: "You may say to yourself, 'My power and the strength of my hands have produced this wealth for me.' But remember the LORD your God, for it is he who gives you the ability to produce wealth" (vv. 17–18).

It was interesting to see that in the three recent seasons when the Chicago Bulls won the world basketball championship, the first thing the team did in the locker room was to huddle together and pray. The TV cameras turned away; the commentators got flustered. But the team paused to acknowledge the God who had gifted them.

Think about it this way: Have you ever gone out of your way to do something especially kind for someone and never received any acknowledgment or thanks? It leaves an empty feeling of disappointment, doesn't it? Well, God has emotions, too.

When we receive from Him without giving thanks or when we take credit that properly belongs to Him, we bring disappointment to the heart of God. And yet the opposite is true, too. When we remember to give God the honor He deserves, we can actually bring a smile to Him.

Luke 17:11–19 describes an encounter between Jesus and ten lepers as He was traveling to Jerusalem. They called to Jesus from a distance, begging for pity, and He graciously responded by healing them. Can you imagine how thrilled they must have been to be freed from that scourge?

And yet only one of them took the time to come over to Jesus and humbly offer thanks. "Where are the other nine?" Jesus asked. Spiritual amnesia, it seems, can set in quickly.

I'll admit that there are times when I've been an amnesia victim. I'm always anxious to ask for God's help, but I wish I was as unfailingly faithful in thanking Him immediately after He comes through for me once again.

Has amnesia ever afflicted you? Would Jesus look at your life and liken you to the grateful leper—or to the forgetful nine who neglected to acknowledge how much they owed to God?

119

Camels and Needles

In a colorful remark that should bring chills to all the Donald Trumps of the world, Jesus said in Matthew 19:24: "It is easier for a camel to go through the eye of a needle than for a rich man to enter the kingdom of God."

He wasn't condemning money. Abraham, Isaac, Jacob, David, and Solomon were wealthy, and they found favor with God. Instead, Jesus' comment was a sobering acknowledgment that money-motivated success tends to create roadblocks between us and God. The illusion of success sends us scurrying after the wrong commodities when we should be pursuing Him. The trap of success isolates us from Him. The cynicism of success blinds us to His likeness in others. And the amnesia of success prompts us to forget the monumental role He plays in our lives.

And yet while camels can't normally fit through a needle's eye, Jesus said a few verses later: "With God, all things are possible." By following God's guidelines for making money ethically and using it generously to help others, we can avoid the regret that comes when we focus on our own short-term success to the exclusion of long-term satisfaction.

I started this chapter with two scenes, both dealing with Donald Trump and his money. I'm going to end with one more scene, this one providing a rare glimpse into Trump's uncertainties.

The scene took place early in 1989, when Trump's bank account was still bulging. At the conclusion of a long day, writer Glenn Plaskin asked Trump the inevitable question about what horizons were left to conquer. "Right now, I'm genuinely enjoying myself," Trump replied. "I work and I don't worry."

"What about death," Plaskin asked. "Don't you worry about dying?"

Trump dealt his stock answer, one that appears in a lot of his interviews. "No," he said. "I'm fatalistic and I protect myself as well as anybody can. I prepare for things."

This time, however, as Trump started walking up the stairs to have dinner with his family, he hesitated for a moment. "No," he said finally. "I don't believe in reincarnation, heaven or hell—but we go someplace."

Again, a pause. "Do you know," he added, "I cannot, for the life of me, figure out where."

Real success, Jesus would say, involves figuring out the truth about that issue once and for all. "What good is it," He asked, "for a man to gain the whole world, and yet lose or forfeit his very self?" (Luke 9:25).

8

What Jesus Would Say to Madalyn Murray O'Hair

How about taking a test? I'll describe someone, and you try to guess who it is.

This individual is an atheist. In fact, this person doesn't just reject the idea of God but also cynically belittles and ridicules those who have faith. To this person, religious people are uncritical thinkers who are wasting their life by engaging in wishful thinking and who revere a book that's filled with glaring inconsistencies, bizarre mythology, and inaccurate history.

This person's denial of God has opened the door to a selfish, vulgar, and often immoral lifestyle. Words like *liar*, *cheater*, *hypocrite*, and *publicity-seeker* only scratch the surface in describing this individual's depth of personal corruption.

Actually, this may not be such a difficult quiz. After all, the person's name is printed on the cover of this book.

It's *Lee Strobel*.

You see, that's an accurate portrait of who I was fifteen years ago. Despite my parents' efforts to introduce me to God, I stubbornly pursued my own path of skepticism and personal pleasure. It wasn't until my agnostic wife, Leslie, became a Christian in 1979 that I slowly became convinced that it would be worthwhile to use my journalism and legal training to systematically investigate the underpinnings of the faith. That two-year journey of spiritual discovery ended up convincing me that the evidence for Christianity is solid, and I received Jesus Christ as the forgiver of my sins and the leader of my life.

I'm mentioning this up front so you'll understand why I have such a passionate interest in people who are still antagonistic toward Christ—including the country's most infamous atheist, Madalyn Murray O'Hair.

America's Most Hated Woman

Lightning flashed in the Maryland sky. The wind howled. Rain pelted her face as a pregnant Madalyn Murray shook her fist toward the heavens and unleashed a torrent of vulgarities as she taunted God to strike her dead for blasphemy.

When she remained untouched, she grew even more defiant. She victoriously turned and declared to her watching family: "You see! You see! If God exists, He would surely have taken up my challenge. I've proved irrefutably that God does not exist!"

That anecdote illustrates the dramatic flair of the former social worker whose 1963 lawsuit succeeded in outlawing prayer and Bible reading in public schools. It's this penchant for the theatrical and bizarre that have kept the founder of American Atheists, Inc., in the public spotlight for more than thirty years as the self-styled "most hated woman in America."

As far back as 1964, a *Saturday Evening Post* profile called her "a strange, immensely complicated woman, full of paradoxes, conflicts, and challenges," and that description remains accurate to this day. Ironies abound with Murray, who married former FBI informant Richard O'Hair in 1965.

She says she rejected God as a youngster, yet she later took her two infant sons to be baptized and she wrote letters from overseas predicting victory in World War II because "God is on our side." She ridicules Christians for believing in an afterlife, but she has reportedly participated in seances to contact the dead. She's famous as a defender of free speech, though she sued a journalist on grounds that he didn't have the right to publish an article about her. She's the person most identified with atheism in this country—saying "I am, in fact, *the* atheist"—and yet she has been vilified by many other nonbelievers for what the *American Rationalist* called her "general abnormal behavior."

"She thoroughly personified the Christian stereotype of an atheist," wrote Lawrence Wright in *Saints and Sinners*. "Rude, impertinent, blasphemous, a destroyer not only of beliefs but of esteemed values—especially sexual values—she popped off like a chain of fireworks in a sanctuary, merrily detonating everything we held dear. It was impossible not to admire her nerve, while at the same time wondering at her apparent compulsion to be loathed."

Undeniably bright and articulate, O'Hair delights in assailing Christianity with barbs seemingly designed to elicit the maximum response. Asked why she's an atheist, she replied, "Because religion is a crutch, and only the crippled need crutches. I can get around perfectly well on my own two feet, and so can everyone else with a backbone and a grain of common sense."

She told *Life* magazine: "We find the Bible to be nauseating, historically inaccurate, replete with the ravings of madmen. We find God to be sadistic, brutal, and a representation of hatred and vengeance. We find the Lord's Prayer to be that muttered by worms groveling for meager existence in a traumatic paranoid world."

To Wright, she railed that "the Pope should be arrested tomorrow for crimes against humanity—just for the fact that he goes out and tells women to breed indiscriminately, to be fruitful and multiply, to get one in the oven tonight. He should be put in a cage."

The Genesis of Disbelief

O'Hair traces her atheism to age twelve or thirteen. "I picked up the Bible and read it from cover to cover one weekend—just as if it were a novel—very rapidly, and I've never gotten over the shock of it," she told *Playboy*. "The miracles, the inconsistencies, the improbabilities, the impossibilities, the wretched history, the sordid sex, the sadism in it—the whole thing shocked me profoundly."

Later, she said, she went to church, where "my first memories are of the minister getting up and accusing us of being full of sin, though he didn't say why; then they would pass the collection plate, and I got it in my mind that this had to do with purification of the soul, that we were being invited to buy expiation from our sins. So I gave it all up. It was too nonsensical."

But her older son believes her atheism stems from her bitterness toward men, especially her lover whose last name—Murray—she took after he fathered her child but refused to marry her. "Mother came to hate the Roman Catholic church and the Pope for preventing her marriage to a man of considerable wealth," her elder son wrote. "My father told her point-blank that it was his devotion to the church that would not permit him to divorce his wife."

He added: "Madalyn Murray was mad at men, and she was mad at God, who is male. Rather than confront her conscience, she determined to deny God's existence and refused to accept any moral constraints. She had to destroy all references to God, because if there were a Deity, then He could make demands on her life."

Whatever the genesis of her disbelief, she was catapulted to fame by the school prayer lawsuit and later started the atheist organization, which is currently operated from Austin, Texas, by O'Hair; her younger son, John Garth Murray; and her granddaughter, Robin Murray. Though there are wide disputes over the group's size, it remains the best-known organization of its type.

Unquestionably O'Hair represents the extreme of atheism. Only about thirteen percent of Americans are agnostic or atheists, and few would be as radical or vitriolic as O'Hair. And so she is part of a very small minority.

But I want to use O'Hair as a representative of all spiritual skeptics as I consider what Jesus might say to her. For instance, you may not be hostile toward the idea of God, but perhaps you're doubtful or confused as to whether He exists. Or maybe you're indifferent toward Him, sort of stuck in spiritual neutral. Or it could be that you have a friend or family member who seems full of objections to the faith.

In any case I think what Jesus would say to O'Hair, though she's on the far end of the disbelief spectrum, might be helpful to you, too.

The Flow of the Facts

Not only does Madalyn Murray O'Hair think God is a fairy tale, but she also doubts whether Jesus ever walked the planet. "There's absolutely no conclusive evidence that He ever really existed, even as a mortal," she told an interviewer. "I don't believe He was a historical figure at all. . . . Until someone proves otherwise, these [Bible] stories must be considered nothing more than folk tales consisting in equal parts of legend and wish fulfillment."

Well, I think the first thing Jesus would do with a skeptic like O'Hair would be to establish up front, right off the bat, the objective reality that He is, indeed, the Son of God, who lived at a point in history, was crucified to pay for the sins of the world, and was raised from the dead three days later. So I think His first statement to her would come directly from the words He spoke in John 8:24: "I am the one I claim to be."

While I've never had an opportunity to discuss this issue with O'Hair, I've talked about it at length with Rob Sherman, who was the national spokesman of her organization. Sherman lives near me and we've become friends over the years. The first time we ate lunch together, I asked him straight out: "Why don't you believe in God?"

"Because," he said, "I don't believe in superstition."

"Hey, that's great!" I replied. "Neither do I. We have something in common!"

I explained that if you look up the word *superstition* in the dictionary, the first definition is "a belief held in spite of evidence to the contrary."

In other words a superstitious person says, "I don't care that the evidence is flowing in one direction; I'm going to swim upstream against the current with what I believe."

Now I'll concede that this is what some people do in the name of religion. They believe all sorts of things despite overwhelming evidence pointing the other way. For example, that's certainly true of Mormonism, where waves of historical, archaeological, and biblical evidence flow against their beliefs.

But that's not what biblical faith is about. Biblical faith says the overall evidence flows in a certain direction, and our faith is going with the current. So our belief that Jesus is who He claimed to be isn't an attempt to swim upstream against history and reality—it's a faith that's consistent with the flow of facts.

"Come and See"

For example, suppose you were the skeptical sort and I offered you a chocolate chip cookie. You might want to check it out before you took a bite. Perhaps you'd look into where the ingredients came from, how it was made, the trustworthiness and reputation of the baker, and the circumstances under which it had been stored. You might want to run some chemical tests or talk to others who have eaten from the same batch to see their reactions.

And if you conclude that the overall evidence indicates that the cookie is safe to eat, then you take a step of faith by eating it. It's not an irrational step, but it's a sensible and logical step that's going in the same direction as the facts.

Similarly, once a person concludes that the overall thrust of the evidence shows that Christianity is true, that's when he takes a reasonable step of faith by putting his trust in Christ. It's like what happened to a skeptic by the name of Nathanael, whose story is recorded by the apostle John.

One day Nathanael's friend, Philip, told him with excitement, "We've found the Messiah who was predicted in all the ancient writings, and His name is Jesus of Nazareth."

But Nathanael wasn't buying it. His response in John 1:46 was basically: "Give me a break! Why should I believe that a guy from a hick town like Nazareth is the Messiah? C'mon—we all know that nothing good ever comes out of Nazareth!"

So Philip simply said, "Come and see." In other words, check Him out for yourself.

Nathanael was at least willing to do that. And guess what he found? When he went to see Jesus, Jesus told him something about his life that He only could have known by supernatural means. Instantly Nathanael responded: "You *are* the Son of God!"

Do you see? Jesus offered the evidence and it convinced Nathanael intellectually that Jesus was God, and then Nathanael was willing to take a step of faith by turning his life over to Christ.

And I think Jesus would say—to Madalyn Murray O'Hair, Rob Sherman, or any other skeptic—the same thing Philip said to Nathanael: "Come and see. Check Me out. See that I am who I claim to be."

An Intellectual Shoot-Out

But where is the evidence that points to Jesus as really being God? Having spent almost two years examining it myself before becoming a believer, I feel highly confident in the strength of the case for Christianity. So my ears perked up one day when Sherman said wistfully to me and my colleague, Mark Mittelberg, "Wouldn't it be great if we could lay out the case for atheism, and your side could lay out the case for Christianity, and we could let the audience decide for themselves?"

"Let's do exactly that," I said. "You go out and find the strongest defender of atheism you can—your best and brightest. We'll bring him here from anywhere in the world. And we'll go out and get a top-notch proponent of Christianity, and we'll have an intellectual shoot-out!"

Isn't that the American way—to fairly present the evidence for both sides and let the listeners determine who's got the strongest case? Our entire judicial system is set up on that model. Besides, Christians have been debating skeptics since the earliest days of the faith, when the apostle Paul clashed with the philosophers in Athens, as described in Acts 17.

Sherman agreed to the idea. Although O'Hair's organization was not affiliated with the debate, Sherman convinced Frank Zindler, O'Hair's good friend and top debater, to represent the atheist side. Zindler is a former professor of geology and biology who writes articles and books for American Atheists, Inc., and has promoted atheism in hundreds of radio and television programs.

Mittelberg, who organized the debate, asked Dr. William Lane Craig, author of numerous books on the evidence for Christianity, to present the Christian case. Craig holds doctorates in philosophy and theology and is a former professor at Trinity Evangelical Divinity School in Deerfield, Illinois.

The showdown was set for June 27, 1993. The place: Willow Creek Community Church in South Barrington, Illinois. The title: "Atheism Versus Christianity—Where Does the Evidence Point?" The news media hyped the debate for weeks as the ultimate clash on the topic. We especially urged nonbelievers to attend.

The atmosphere that night was electric. So many people converged on the church that traffic became gridlocked in the area. The church's auditorium seats 4,500 people, but 7,778 overflowed the facility, with many ending up watching the program on video monitors in six different rooms. The debate was carried live on more than one hundred radio stations around the country.

I served as moderator, allowing both Zindler and Craig time to present their main cases and then gave them three other opportunities to respond to each other's remarks. Afterward, following remarks by Mittelberg and Sherman, questions were taken from the audience.

What the public didn't know is that in the basement beneath the stage, in a small room, a group of Christians quietly gathered. They were committed to praying during the entire program that the evidence for Christ would be proclaimed loud and clear.

And their prayers were answered.

Showdown Over the Evidence

Craig spelled out five powerful arguments for God and Christianity. First, that the so-called "Big Bang" at the beginning of the universe clearly points toward a Creator. Second, that the universe exhibits the unmistakable handiwork of an intelligent designer. Third, that our objective moral values are evidence that there's a God, since only He could establish an ultimate standard of right and wrong. Fourth, that the historical evidence for Christ's resurrection—including the empty tomb, eyewitness accounts, and origin of the Christian faith—establish the divinity of Jesus. And, fifth, that God can be immediately known and experienced by those who seek Him.

Despite Craig's repeated challenges, Zindler balked at offering an affirmative case for atheism. Instead, Zindler charged that biological evolution "is the death knell of Christianity"; that there's no convincing evidence that Jesus actually lived; that the existence of evil argues against God; and that some biblical references are inaccurate or conflict with science.

After Craig corrected many of Zindler's inaccuracies about the Bible, he then proceeded to turn Zindler's main arguments against him. He pointed out that if evolution did occur despite the prohibitive odds against it, then it must have been a miracle and therefore evidence for the existence of God! As for evil in the world, Craig pointed out, "No logical inconsistency has ever been demonstrated between the two statements 'God exists' and 'evil exists.'" Besides, he added, in a deeper sense the presence of evil "actually demonstrates God's existence because without God there wouldn't be any [moral] foundation for calling anything evil."

At the end of the debate, we asked the audience to vote for which side had presented the strongest case. I stressed to everyone that they should set aside their personal beliefs and vote only for which side had laid out the most compelling evidence that night.

It was clear to me that Christianity had thoroughly trounced atheism. The only question was by what margin. When I was handed the results to announce, I found that the vote had been virtually unanimous. Ninety-seven percent declared that the Christian case prevailed!

A cynic might object, "Well, of course—this took place in a church." However, we asked people to record their spiritual position *before* the debate and then *after* they heard the evidence. Of the 632 people who said they were definitely *not* Christians, an overwhelming eighty-two percent of them concluded that the evidence offered for Christianity was definitely the most compelling.

And—get this!—forty-seven of the people who had walked in as unbelievers walked out as believers! *The evidence for Christ was so strong that they became modern-day Nathanaels!*

By the way, nobody became an atheist.

The Reality of the Resurrection

The results of that debate aren't a fluke. A few years earlier, one of the world's top philosophical atheists, Dr. Anthony Flew, author of *The Presumption of Atheism* and fifteen other books, debated Dr. Gary Habermas, a Christian professor and noted defender of the faith. Their topic: Did Jesus really rise from the dead?

After all, the Resurrection is the linchpin of Christianity. "If Christ has not been raised, your faith is futile; you are still in your sins," the apostle Paul wrote in 1 Corinthians 15:17. In other words, no Resurrection, no Christianity.

For two intensive days, Habermas and Flew pelted each other with their best evidence and bombarded each other with their most convincing arguments. When the smoke cleared, a panel of five judges—independent university professors from a variety of backgrounds—issued its verdict. Four panelists said the Christian won. Only one wasn't sure; he called it a draw.

Listeners were amazed by the strength of the historical case for the Resurrection. One judge said the evidence "is strong enough to lead reasonable minds to conclude that Christ did, indeed, rise from the dead." Another said the atheistic position was shockingly weak, and added: "I would think it was time that I began to take the Resurrection seriously."

This didn't surprise me. And I'm not surprised by story after story of doctors, lawyers, engineers, professors, and others whose doubts about Christ have been dispelled by a thorough examination of the evidence. I know one cynical investigative journalist who took some courses on Christianity just so he would be better equipped to debunk the faith. Instead, he not only ended up becoming a Christian, but he now teaches a weekly Bible study for skeptics!

I'd encourage anyone with doubts to sincerely check out the claims of Christ for himself. There's no shortage of top-notch resources available. Remember the promise of Jeremiah 29:13: "You will seek me and find me when you seek me with all your heart."

Seeking and Saving the Lost

After Jesus established who He is, I think another thing He would say to Madalyn Murray O'Hair or any other nonbeliever would be this: "You matter to Me, and you should matter to My followers, too."

Jesus said it was His mission to seek and save those who are spiritually lost. To drive home that point, He told three rapid-fire stories in Luke 15 about a lost sheep, a lost coin, and a lost son as a way of emphasizing how important wayward people are to Him.

But it took an incident with my daughter, Alison, to help me really appreciate this. One Saturday afternoon Leslie and I took Alison, who was then seven, to a small theme park outside Chicago called Pirate's Cove. The three-acre facility was packed with people.

As we strolled through the grounds, Leslie and I became immersed in conversation. Then, all of a sudden, she looked around and said, "Where's Alison?"

"I don't know," I said. "I thought you had your eye on her."

"I thought *you* did," she said with panic in her voice.

Immediately we realized that we hadn't seen Alison for several minutes. We quickly scanned the immediate area, but there was no sign of her. I'll tell you what—my heart jumped into my throat! I broke out in a cold sweat.

We decided to make a systematic sweep of the park. Starting at one end, we began searching frantically for our daughter. We looked on the rides, behind bushes, in the washrooms. We reached the other end of the park—but we still hadn't found her. I felt like crying! I was nauseated and light-headed with fear.

The park's exit was wide open. She easily could have wandered outside—or been abducted. I sprinted into the parking lot, but again there was no sign of her. Now I was absolutely terrified. I ran up to the ticket-taker and shouted in her face: "My daughter's gone! You've got to do something!"

If anything like that has ever happened to you, then you're familiar with the emotions that surged through me. You love your child so much that you want him or her to be safe with you.

And on the authority of Scripture, I can tell you this: *God feels those same kind of emotions toward every person who is*

133

spiritually lost. In fact, because His love is even greater than what we feel toward our children, His emotions are even more powerful than what you and I experience.

And I think Jesus would say to Madalyn Murray O'Hair, "You've had two sons. You've raised a granddaughter. Can you imagine how you would have felt if any of them had been lost like Alison? Well, that gives you a small taste of how I feel about you."

Fortunately our story had a happy ending. As it turned out, Alison had wandered into an exhibit that we hadn't searched because it looked like it was locked. She came walking out with the crowd a while later, and when I saw her, I scooped her into my arms and hugged and kissed her. I felt like throwing a party!

It reminded me of Luke 15:10, which says: "There is rejoicing in the presence of the angels of God over one sinner who repents."

A celestial celebration breaks out whenever any skeptic realizes the truth about God!

Despite her acerbic cynicism, I believe Madalyn Murray O'Hair still matters to God in ways she can't even begin to appreciate. If there's room in God's kingdom for Saul of Tarsus, who actually helped murder Christians, then I think there's room for O'Hair, who has merely wounded them with words. The Bible says in 2 Peter 3:9: "The Lord is patient with you, not wanting anyone to perish, but everyone to come to repentance."

At the same time, I believe that God has some expectations for His followers. He wants us to be willing to extend grace to skeptics, even when it goes against the grain of how we feel toward them.

Why in the world should I have compassion for a person like O'Hair even though she may not deserve it? Because Jesus Christ had compassion on me—and *I* definitely *didn't* deserve it.

Do Skeptics Matter to Us?

Let's face it: Atheists can be unpopular. O'Hair has called herself the most despised person in the country, and one Chicago newspaper called Sherman "the guy many people love to hate."

Some people have reacted bitterly against them because of their inflammatory language. Sherman says people claiming to be

Christians have threatened him and his family, and that he has received harassing phone calls from time to time. O'Hair says she has received hate-filled letters and been the target of vandalism.

Do you see what can happen? When we begin railing against "those atheists" or "those godless humanists," they cease in our minds to be individuals who matter to God. Suddenly they become a monolithic mass of faceless enemies—and in a war, there's no fraternizing with the other side. We distance ourselves from them. Walls of suspicion and distrust are built.

But Jesus said in Matthew 10:16: "Be as shrewd as snakes and as innocent as doves." We have to be wise enough to vigorously oppose the political and judicial efforts of atheists when they try to remove the thread of God that is woven so tightly into the moral fabric of this country. If that thread were ever removed, our morality as a nation would completely unravel.

And we must be shrewd enough to look beyond O'Hair's stated goal of merely wanting to separate church and state and see her objective for what she once admitted it really is: "I want to be able to walk down any street in America and not see a cross or any other sign of religion."

But while we should oppose attacks on religious freedom, we should also be gentle enough to continue to pray for and reach out to spiritual skeptics as individuals who matter to God.

I know how I feel toward atheists. I've experienced firsthand the emptiness of atheism and the fulfillment of Christianity. So I don't want to beat atheists into the ground; I want to find common ground so we can talk about truth. And common ground gets built on compassion and reason, not on harsh attacks.

Think about that Roman soldier who was assigned to help crucify a religious rabble-rouser named Jesus nearly two thousand years ago. What would have happened if Jesus had scowled down from the cross and angrily declared: "You're headed for hell, buddy! Turn or burn, you godless pagan! You're going to suffer in eternity for this!" Don't you think that would have only further hardened that centurion's heart?

Instead, a gentle Jesus, despite the pain of torture, demonstrated incredible kindness by saying, "Father, forgive them, for they do not know what they are doing" (Luke 23:34). That supernatural display of tender mercy—as well as the accompanying evidence of earth tremors at the time of Jesus' death—pierced the heart of that soldier. "Surely he was the Son of God!" he finally exclaimed in Matthew 27:54.

I've seen Christians only harden skeptics by their mean-spirited words of denunciation. And yet I've also seen onetime cynics whose hearts have become yielded to God after a Christian has offered them reasoned evidence for God in the context of a loving and caring relationship.

That's the approach I believe Jesus would encourage His people to take.

Becoming a Spiritual Seeker

Another statement Jesus might make to O'Hair would be a quotation from the Old Testament, where Joshua said, "Choose for yourselves this day whom you will serve" (Josh. 24:15).

You see, ultimately the choice is O'Hair's to make. In Revelation 3:20, Jesus says, "I stand at the door and knock." Every person has a choice: Ignore His knocking or open the door.

Now it's true that Jesus could put His foot in the door and force it open. He could try to compel people to love Him—but that wouldn't really evoke love on our part, would it? Love has to involve a choice. For there to be real love, there has to be the option of not loving. And so God gave us the capacity to choose, so that we might make the decision to love Him.

He said, in effect: "If you choose to live apart from Me during your life, I'll honor that decision, and I won't impose Myself on you. But you need to know this: I'll honor that choice for all eternity, and that means living apart from Me forever." And none of us can comprehend the horror of endlessly living apart from any influence of God.

But Jesus says, "If you choose to receive My free gift of forgiveness now, I'll begin a rich and real and rewarding relationship with You that will stretch throughout eternity." And none of us can comprehend the incredible fulfillment of being in God's pure presence forever.

Sometimes Christians feel frustrated because they'd like to make the choice for someone else. But they can't. And they're not responsible for others beyond clearly communicating the truth of God to them. It's each person's decision, and people are different in how receptive they are toward God.

For instance, it has been said we could divide the world into three camps. Camp A would consist of people who have sought God and found Him. Camp B would be people who are seeking God and will find Him. (Since the Bible says that all those who sincerely seek God will find Him, everybody in Camp B eventually ends up in Camp A.) Finally, there's Camp C, consisting of people who aren't seeking God at all.

People ensconced in Camp C may be close-minded, afraid, or indifferent toward God. But whatever their reason for being there, Camp C doesn't hold much of a future. Unless God dramatically intervenes, Camp C is a dead end.

And yet there's no downside for those in Camp C who decide to move to Camp B. There's nothing to lose by praying the seeker's prayer, which says, "God, I don't know if You're there, but if You are, I sincerely want to find You. If You're there, draw me to Yourself, and help me discover the truth about You."

Look at it this way: If there's no God, you haven't lost anything. But if there is, you've got everything to gain.

A Life Without God

There's a businessman named Bill who grew up in a home where people were proud residents of Camp C. When it came to God, their minds were clamped shut. In fact, his mother told him, "I don't care if you become a drug addict or a bank robber or if you bring home a boyfriend instead of a girlfriend. There's just one thing I don't want you to do in life—become a Christian."

As a young man, Bill adopted a lifestyle consistent with his atheism. In other words, since there's no God to set an ultimate standard of right or wrong, morals become what feels good or what you can get away with.

So in his quest for pleasure, Bill lived a life of sexual conquests, and he suffered the consequences through marriages and relationships that fell apart. In his desire for money to buy things to make himself happy, he worked to the point of exhaustion. In an attempt to escape the despair of thinking that there's no real purpose to life and nothing beyond the grave, he drank heavily and got involved with drugs.

But even in the midst of all that—or perhaps *because* of all that—he became willing to open his mind just enough to move from Camp C to Camp B. One day he looked at his life and prayed to the God he had always rejected: "Please, get me out of this mess!"

After being startled one night by a dream, he went to an all-night bookstore near his home in San Francisco. Under a stack of pornographic magazines he found a Bible—the book he had always criticized, but which he had never honestly tried to understand. He went home and began reading the biography of Jesus as recorded by the historian Luke.

And he became convinced of three things. First, that Jesus is who He claimed to be. Second, that he mattered to God. And, third, that he needed to choose who he was going to serve.

Choosing Christ

So he made his decision on January 25, 1980. After three decades of the hollowness of atheism, he said a prayer that wasn't very eloquent, but which expressed his heart. "Jesus," he said, "I want to be with You instead of what I'm doing!" He admitted his sinfulness and asked Jesus to forgive him and lead his life. In other words he graduated to Camp A.

Over time Jesus changed him in a radical way. He was able to break free from alcohol and drugs and to rebuild his life and relationships. His whole attitude changed, and instead of living a life focused on himself, he developed a desire to share Christ's compassion with others. He began helping atheists work through their spiritual confusion, and he started a ministry to provide medical supplies to relieve the suffering of refugees from Communist countries.

He even learned to love his mother. He realized that she was just a sinner like him who was engaged in the wishful thinking that there's no God because she didn't want to be held morally accountable for the life she was leading.

You see, Bill's full name is William J. Murray, and he's the oldest son of Madalyn Murray O'Hair. In his book *My Life Without*

God, he describes how his mother used him as the plaintiff in the Supreme Court case that outlawed school prayer, and he recounts his amazing pilgrimage from atheism to God.

After he became a Christian, he sent a letter to be published in several newspapers. "As I now look back over thirty-three years of life wasted without faith in God," he wrote, "I pray only that I can, with His help, right some of the wrong and evil I have caused through my lack of faith."

William Murray opened his mind enough to become a sincere seeker. Like Nathanael, he came and he saw. You have to wonder whether his mother will ever have the similar courage to check out Jesus with an open mind.

And what about you? If you're plagued by doubts or still trying to determine if there's a God who cares about you, are you willing to take the time to explore the facts for yourself? Hebrews 11:6 says about God, "He rewards those who earnestly seek Him."

After all, there's no downside to becoming a spiritual seeker, but I'll tell you what I found out: There's a terrific upside.

9

What Jesus Would Say to *Murphy Brown*

Fictional newswoman Murphy Brown wasn't the first television character to get pregnant outside of marriage.

It's been happening for more than thirty years, dating back to a 1960 episode of the soap opera *As the World Turns*. Since then, according to the *New York Times*, Mary Jo in *Designing Women*, Carla on *Cheers*, Maddie on *Moonlighting*, Susannah on *Thirtysomething*, Maggie on *Baby Talk*, K.C. on *China Beach*, Jenna on *Dallas*, and Emma on *Falcon Crest* have been among the unwed characters who have either had or tried to have babies in recent years.

That doesn't include Gina on *Santa Barbara*. In one of TV's more distasteful plots, she pilfered her former husband's sperm from a sperm bank and later gave birth in an animal hospital!

But none of these incidents sparked the kind of furor that erupted when wisecracking, politically correct Murphy Brown, played by actress Candice Bergen, announced she was pregnant.

To this day the debate over unwed motherhood remains hotly contested, fueled from time to time by such incidents as a Texas school trying to ban pregnant students from the cheerleading squad and state legislators trying to halt further welfare payments for unmarried women who bear more than one child. Seldom has a TV character focused so much attention on such an important political and social issue.

So let's go back to the inception of the Murphy Brown controversy. It started when she had a fling with her former husband. After learning she was pregnant, he opted to go try to save the Brazilian rain forest rather than assume the role of a father. Murphy—who said she wasn't interested in marriage anyway—decided to keep the baby and raise him herself.

Murphy Gets Slam-Dunked

Thirty-eight million people watched Murphy give birth to little Avery, but it was then-Vice President Dan Quayle who really catapulted her to notoriety. In a widely reported speech, he said that a "poverty of values" is leading to more and more fatherless families, causing our social structure to unravel, especially in the inner cities.

He said Hollywood shares the blame. "Bearing babies irresponsibly is simply wrong," he said. "Failure to support children one has fathered is wrong. We must be unequivocal about this. It doesn't help matters when prime time TV has Murphy Brown—a character who supposedly epitomizes today's intelligent, highly paid, professional woman—mocking the importance of a father by bearing a child alone and calling it just another 'lifestyle choice.'"

Quayle's speech became front-page news. "Murphy Has a Baby; Quayle Has a Cow" screamed one headline. Said another: "Quayle to Murphy Brown: You Tramp!"

Some jumped to Murphy's defense, saying it was time America admitted that the traditional two-parent family is as outdated as *Ozzie and Harriet*. They said there are many species of equally valid lifestyles, including families that are "father-optional." Some suggested it was sexist to insist a father needs to be in the home, adding that anyone as educated and affluent as

Murphy Brown would have no trouble raising a well-adjusted child on her own.

But what slant might Jesus put on this issue? Certainly He'd have a viewpoint, wouldn't He? After all, the trend of fatherless families is a vitally important sociological phenomenon.

Consider the statistics. One out of every four American children lives in a single-parent home. And the trend is accelerating; the number of one-parent families nearly tripled in the last twenty years. This development crosses racial and economic lines. One out of every five white children, one out of every three Hispanic children, and one out of every two African-American children are being raised by one parent. The rate is increasing fastest among whites.

And get this: A majority of children born today—60 percent of them—will live at least part of their life in a single-parent family before they turn eighteen. You can be sure of one thing: Either directly or indirectly, the fallout is going to affect you personally.

Jesus to Murphy: *You Matter!*

So given the magnitude of the issue, I'm convinced Jesus would have something to say about it. But would He slam-dunk Murphy like some people have? Or would He concede that two-parent families are dinosaurs from the past as some of her supporters have claimed?

Based on the conversations He had with people in biblical times, I think we can be pretty confident of at least three things He might say to Murphy Brown if she were a real person facing unwed motherhood. First, I believe he would say this:

"Murphy, before we talk about anything else, we need to get something straight right at the outset: *You matter to Me, no matter what.* You've got to understand that you're a masterpiece of My creation, you're imprinted with My very image, and you're valuable to Me regardless of what you have or haven't done."

From cover to cover, the Bible screams the message that people matter to God. And God didn't just say it—He demonstrated it by sending His Son to be sacrificed so that we might become reconciled with Him.

Isn't it amazing that God would go out on a limb by declaring His great love for us and then wait—*quietly, patiently*—for our response? For *your* response. But He does.

Then after telling Murphy how much she means to Him, Jesus might say something like this: "Because you matter to Me, I want to help you avoid doing things that will harm yourself. That's why I set boundaries for your behavior. You see, people often misunderstand My motives. I didn't give you moral boundaries to frustrate you or cramp your style or punish you. One reason I established reasonable boundaries was to try to keep you safe from harm and to protect you from hurting yourself and others."

The Benefits of Boundaries

The Bible makes it clear what kind of behavior is in bounds and what's out of bounds, and that sex apart from marriage is definitely out of bounds. You see, Jesus understands the turmoil that nonmarital sex can create in the lives of people who matter to Him.

He understands the emotional devastation that people can suffer when they get so intimately involved with someone outside the security of marriage. He understands the loneliness that can result when intimacy is followed by abandonment.

Jesus understands the guilt that can haunt people after sexual encounters that burn bright for a few moments but then turn cold. He understands how a sense of shame can discourage people from pursuing the kind of spiritual relationship they need with God. He understands the devastating risks of sexually transmitted diseases.

He understands that when pregnancy occurs, so often it's the father who takes off and the mother who is left with the grueling task of raising the child alone. And He wants to protect the people He loves from having to go through any of that.

Friends, God lovingly set reasonable boundaries for our behavior to benefit us, because we matter so much to Him. And yet—this is the truly incredible part—even when we breach those boundaries, as Murphy certainly did, we *still* matter.

In fact, the apostle Paul once wrote to some Christians in the city of Corinth and defined some out-of-bounds behavior—like nonmarital sex—just so there would be no confusion.

Then in the very next verse, 1 Corinthians 6:11, he followed that by saying, in effect: "Let's admit something here—there was a time when some of you were involved with this very kind of behavior. But look at what's happened! God didn't abandon you; He has accepted you as His children because you've asked for His forgiveness through His Son, Jesus Christ."

And if Jesus came face-to-face with a real-life Murphy Brown, I think He'd say, "I care about you so much that I was willing to pay the penalty for your sin so that you wouldn't have to. And when you come to Me with sincerity and express regret for your mistake and then ask for forgiveness, I'll tell you what—*I'll absolutely shower you with it.*"

Facing up to our out-of-bounds behavior is a lot easier when we know that God's desire isn't retribution, but reconciliation. It's forgiveness and a healed relationship with Him. Because of that, there's no question in my mind that Jesus would say to a real-life Murphy Brown: "Forgiveness is yours for the asking, because you matter to Me, *no matter what.*"

The Perils of Single Parenthood

I think Jesus would follow that up with a second important statement: "Your child matters to Me, too, and you need to know that he's at great risk. For his sake and for yours, you need to understand that."

You see, God cares so much about children and meeting their needs to be nurtured, taught, and loved that He designed families from the very beginning with a mother *and* a father. Both are crucial to the child's development. Yet there are more than ten million single-family homes in this country, with the father missing in ninety percent of them. Think of the impact that's having on the children.

For the son, it means his father's not there to be an everyday role model, to help him understand what it means to grow into a responsible man, to shape his character and values in ways that only a father can. And too often, these sons end up feeling compelled to go out and prove their manhood in self-destructive ways.

For the daughter, it means her father's not there on a consistent basis to reinforce his affirmation of her and his love for her.

With that critically important component of her upbringing missing, she may be haunted by uncertainties about herself. Unfortunately, many times these young women end up in a fruitless search for male acceptance through early sexual encounters.

That's why I shake my head when I see a headline like this one, which appeared in a major newspaper: "Who Needs a Man? Unmarried and Uninvolved, More Single Women Are Looking to Casual Acquaintances and Fertility Clinics to Conceive Babies They Plan to Raise Alone."

Shortly after that headline appeared, another newspaper featured this story: "New Census Figures Show Further Deterioration Of U.S. Families." What's at the root of that deterioration? An expert in the article pinpointed the problem as being "the growing social acceptance of a woman having a child without getting married."

One thing is clear: When we abandon God's formula for the family by subtracting a dad *or* a mom from the equation of a child's life, the results can be tragic.

The Fallout from Fatherless Homes

Now, I know that many single mothers didn't deliberately choose that lifestyle. They were forced into that role against their will. They had no choice but to escape an abusive or intolerable marital situation or they were abandoned by their spouse, and they're victims in the truest sense of the word. A lot of them are heroines who are doing a terrific job of raising their children despite difficult circumstances.

But we can't ignore that the overall statistics establish convincingly that children raised in one-parent homes are at risk in virtually every area of life—emotionally, intellectually, physically, behaviorally, and financially. In fact, let me machine-gun you with some very scary statistics:

- Eighty percent of teenagers in psychiatric hospitals are from one-parent homes.
- Three out of four teenage suicides occur in one-parent families.

- Regardless of race or income, kids from single-parent homes are up to forty percent more likely to suffer physical health problems and up to thirty percent more likely to be injured in accidents.
- Children raised by a single parent are six times more likely to end up mired in permanent poverty.
- If you visit a prison and interview inmates convicted of violent sex crimes, you'll find that six out of ten are from one-parent families. Talk to teenagers charged with murder and you'll find that seventy-five percent of them are from broken homes.
- Children reared by unmarried mothers are three times more likely to fail a grade in school, three times more likely to end up expelled or suspended, and twice as likely to end up in juvenile jails.
- One study of eighteen thousand students documented that children from single-parent homes did worse in school and got into more trouble than others. In fact, kids from poor homes with two parents outperformed kids from rich homes with only one parent!
- Another major study examined eleven thousand crimes committed in three U.S. cities. Get this—researchers couldn't find any correlation between the crimes and either the race of the offender or the defendant's economic status. But what they did find was a definite connection between crime and the offenders having been raised in "father-absent households."

I could go on and on, but the message is chillingly clear: *Raising children alone can be hazardous to their health!*

And I think Jesus would say: "Don't you see? I designed families to have both a mother and a father for good reasons. These statistics provide frightening evidence of what can happen when you stray out of bounds. I'm trying to protect your children from this kind of fallout."

The Quest for Values

Few things have caused me to fear for this country as much as these statistics concerning single-parent families. I'm frightened because the American family is unraveling at an alarming rate. More and more fathers and mothers are trading in their families in a selfish quest for self-fulfillment elsewhere, and fewer and fewer married

147

couples these days are willing to make the effort to work through marital problems to try to save their relationship.

As a result, we're producing a generation of children who are emotionally scarred, and they, in turn, are leaving their children scarred. Society is beginning to reel from the resulting poverty, despair, and delinquency. Increasingly, people are asking, "What are we going to do to shore up the American family?" And the common response is, "We need family values!" It has almost become a cliché. But as *Newsweek* asked in a particularly astute headline: "Whose Values?"

In other words many Americans agree that we need a rejuvenation of values in our families. But the real question is, "Whose values are we going to adopt?" The values of those who are pushing for same-sex marriages? The values of those who see nothing wrong with "father-optional families"? The values of Hollywood, which bombards TV viewers with more than ten thousand sexual incidents a year, ninety-three percent of which are outside marriage? *Whose* values?

I wonder if Jesus might answer that question by asking a question of His own: "Whose values but God's really work?"

Whose values but God's really safeguard children and nurture them into healthy and well-adjusted adulthood? Whose values but God's offer the reasonable boundaries needed to protect adults from the harmful consequences of their own behavior? The statistics I just cited show conclusively that straying out of the bounds God has set in the area of sexuality and mom-and-dad families puts children—and, ultimately, society itself—at grave risk.

In the end I don't think that even Murphy Brown's brains or money are going to be enough by themselves to shield her son from the long-term fallout of living day-by-day without a dad.

Jesus Throws a Lifeline

So what's to become of the Murphy Browns of the world? Faced with these harsh realities, what is any woman or man going to do if they're cast in the role of raising a family alone?

I think the answer is in another statement that Jesus might make to Murphy Brown: "Murphy, I'm here to help both you and your child beat the odds."

148

It's in God's heart to want to help. In fact, Psalm 10:14 contains a wonderful description of God as being "the helper of the fatherless." In short, the odds facing single-parent families may be great, but God is greater.

"You're going to encounter some monumental challenges as a single mom," I could imagine Jesus telling Murphy. "But I'll help you face them because you and your child matter to Me. I'll be available to encourage you in the midst of your distress, to give you wisdom when you're not sure which way to turn, to give you patience when you're at the end of your rope, and to give you perseverance when you think you can't go on.

"What's more, I'll give you a practical guidebook for how to raise your son into a well-adjusted man and lead him toward a relationship with Me that will revolutionize his life. And I can put you into a community of My people who will put flesh and blood on My love for you."

Does that sound merely like a sugary, feel-good, pie-in-the-sky kind of sentiment to you? If so, you ought to read the words of some single parents at our church who have written about how God has repeatedly come through for them. Here's a sample:

> Throughout my adolescence and young adult life, I struggled with faith and I felt abandoned by my family and God. I taught myself that I was alone in the world and had to learn to survive in this manner.
>
> As a young single mother, these feelings were even more pronounced. I was cynical about faith in God and considered Him a crutch. The futility of this struggle reached a culmination after several years of seeing my relationship with my son deteriorate. At this point, I needed more than a crutch—I needed a wheelchair!
>
> I prayed for the first time in years: "Father, I can't do this anymore. I'm lost, I'm scared, and I don't have the answers. I'm turning it all over to You." Now I know He's my Savior. He has proved to be my comfort, my guidance, my Father.

Here is a woman who is absolutely convinced that God has made a concrete, everyday difference in her life, as He has in the life of another single parent, who wrote: "I actually feel the presence of God's inner peace in spite of the difficulty of my situation.

He is faithful to His word. God has never turned away from me. As the Bible promises, He is definitely there, making my paths straight."

God's Caring Community

Not only have these single mothers drawn strength and guidance from their relationship with Christ, but they've also found that His church provides a tangible expression of His love for them.

Yet even as I write these words, I know that not too many years ago, when I was a cynic, I would have scoffed at that statement. I used to drive by churches and think, *What an incredible monument to the ego of men! What a waste of brick and mortar!* I didn't see the *real* church—people serving and loving each other in the name of Jesus.

If you're a skeptic today, let me use the example of just one church as an illustration of how a community of believers has turned the love of Christ into concrete action for single parents— who are among the neediest people in our society. Admittedly our church is large and consequently has many people mobilized to help others. But this will give you a flavor of the kind of actions being taken by communities of God's people around the world.

For instance, several attenders of our church got together and said, "Our hearts go out to unmarried women who are pregnant, so let's help them navigate this crisis in their life. We'll volunteer to walk alongside of them, to support them, to encourage them, to build into them spiritually, and to help them problemsolve. We want to be there for them for the long haul." These folks ended up creating a ministry called "Alone and Pregnant" to do just that.

Another group had some meetings and said, "We love kids, and we know that children in single-parent homes need a role model—someone who's the same gender as the missing parent. So we'll offer our time to get together with those kids and sort of fill in, as best we can, for the absent parent."

Then some others said, "We love children, too, and we know that kids who lose a parent through death or divorce go through all kinds of emotional difficulties. Sometimes they blame themselves for their parents' breakup; often they're tied into emotional knots. So what we'll do is create a safe and spiritual environment where we can help them process their loss. We'll call it the Rainbows Ministry."

Another group said, "God has gifted us as teachers, and we've got some relevant life experiences, so here's what we'll do—we'll put on regular workshops and seminars on parenting skills and divorce recovery to help single parents get on the path to emotional and spiritual wholeness. We'll help them come to grips with the dynamics that caused their first relationship to fail so they can prevent the same thing from happening again."

Some others said, "Somebody needs to take care of the kids while their parents are at these seminars, so we'll be glad to do that. We'll call it the Oasis Ministry, because that's what we want it to be for them—a safe and fun oasis in their lives."

Then another group said, "Single-parent families need time for recreation, but they don't have much money. So we'll put together retreats, activities, and camping trips that are inexpensive and safe so everyone can get together and have some healthy fun."

Others said, "We know that a lot of single moms struggle financially. When their car breaks down, sometimes they can't afford to fix it and they might lose their job as a result. But God has gifted us with our hands, and so we'll offer our time and skills to fix the cars of needy single parents for free."

From Parties to Parking

Then some teenagers from the church got together and said, "Lots of kids in single-parent families have a depressing Christmas. So why don't we sort of adopt a bunch of families, and we'll cut them a Christmas tree; we'll save up some money to buy the kids food and presents, and we'll come to their homes to throw a big party, because we care about them."

I could go on and on, but one of my favorites involves our church parking lot. Have you ever noticed how at most buildings, such as corporate headquarters, parking places are status symbols? Prime spaces located closest to the entrance have "reserved" stamped all over them—reserved for the president, reserved for the treasurer, reserved for the chairman of the board.

Except for handicapped spaces, there has never been any preferred parking at our church—not for the senior pastor, not for the staff, not for the board of directors. Not for me, either, although I was once offered a reserved spot in the back row!

Then one day someone said at a meeting, "You know, single moms get pushed around too much in society. Nobody gives them a break. And when they come here for services, lots of times they have to park way in the back and trudge through the lot with one or two or three kids in tow, and the thing is, there's nobody around to help. My heart goes out to them. Can't we do something?"

So the church decided to take the best parking places and designate them "One-Parent Parking," just to give single moms a break. It's a small gesture, but it sends a big message: "You matter to God, your children matter to God, and we want you to know that you matter to us, too."

On top of all of this, guess what else happens at the church? Single parents themselves get involved in ministries to help each other, and then they even turn around and serve people with different needs.

This is the beauty of the body of Christ at work! There's nothing in the world like His church. Name one other institution that undergirds hurting families and hurting people the way God's community does. God wants His church to be a place of hope and healing for single parents and others who are fighting the odds stacked against them.

I think Jesus would say to a real-life Murphy Brown: "Let Me and My people help you. You might not need the financial support that most single moms do, but you and your child will need spiritual and emotional support. Get involved in a community of My people and let them begin to alleviate some of your needs, even as you discover the fulfillment that comes when I use you as My conduit to flow My love to others."

That's the slant I think Jesus would put on the Murphy Brown controversy. I think His message to single moms would be hopeful, not hostile. And maybe part of His imaginary talk with Murphy has provided some hope for you, too.

Taking a Step Yourself

Maybe you're beating yourself up over a time that you strayed out of bounds sexually. You merely needed to be reminded that you matter to God no matter what, and that the road toward forgiveness and a clean conscience begins with a simple, sincere prayer. Isaiah 1:18 says, "Though your sins are like scarlet, they shall be as white as snow; though they are red as crimson, they shall be like wool." First John 1:9 assures us, "If we confess our sins, he is faithful and just and will forgive us our sins and purify us from all unrighteousness."

Or perhaps you've been feeling lured from your family by a quest for self-fulfillment, or you're tempted to give up on a marriage even though there's still a spark of life left in it. You just needed to get hit between the eyes with the scary truth about the risks you'd be exposing your children to. Aren't they worth another effort at making your marriage work? Can't you make one more attempt—perhaps with the help of a minister or Bible-believing Christian counselor—to reconcile with your spouse?

It could be that you're not a single parent at all, but someone involved in a church that, for whatever reason, has turned a deaf ear to their cries for help. Unfortunately some churches shame unwed moms with a harsh, judgmental attitude rather than expressing Christ's compassion toward them. Perhaps you need to go to God and ask His forgiveness for allowing the church's heart to grow cold toward people who matter to Him. Then maybe you should brainstorm with others at church, asking, "How can we share the love of Christ with the needy single parents among us?"

Or it could be that you're a person who God has blessed with financial resources, and as you were reading about the needs of children in broken homes, you thought to yourself, *God could use me to make a real difference in their lives.* Is there a one-parent family down the block whose suffering could be softened by an anonymous card of encouragement stuffed with money? Jesus said in Matthew 6:1–4 that when you give to those in need, do it secretly. "Then," He said, "your Father, who sees what is done in secret, will reward you."

Or, finally, maybe you're a single parent who is feeling battered and overwhelmed by the world. More than anything, you might need to say to God what I quoted that other unwed mother as saying: "Father, I can't do this anymore. I'm lost, I'm scared, and I don't have the answers. I'm turning it all over to You."

You can have the utmost confidence that God will be "the helper of the fatherless." In fact, that phrase comes from a poem written by King David, who himself fathered a child out of wedlock and who subsequently experienced the fullness of God's forgiveness.

Actually I can't think of a more appropriate way to end this chapter on Murphy Brown than to quote David's closing words in Psalm 10:

> Lord, you know the hopes of humble people. Surely you will hear their cries and comfort their hearts by helping them. You will be with the orphans and all who are oppressed, so that mere earthly man will terrify them no longer. (LB)

10

Top Ten Things Jesus Would Say to
David Letterman

10. Sorry—Johnny gets the 11:30 slot in eternity.

9. Thanks for not leaving New York City. Contrary to popular opinion, God hasn't either.

8. In hell, that woman breaks into your house *every* night.

7. Some things are just plain hard to explain, even for Me. Predestination versus free will, for instance. And your hair.

6. When I talk about King David, I'm not always referring to your ratings.

5. Behave yourself, or I'll reveal to the world that you were Chip on *My Three Sons*.

4. No, Dave, I *won't* fix it so you get free HBO.

3. Let's face it: You owe God some credit for coming up with history's first Top Ten list.

2. You think it's fun to be omniscient? Hey, every once in a while I'd like to hear a punch line that I didn't already know.

1. No, God isn't dead; He's just banned from the networks.

11

What Jesus Would Say to You... and Me

During his five years as a prisoner in North Vietnam, Major F. J. Harold Kushner encountered a twenty-four-year-old Marine who had made a deal with his captors.

The soldier agreed to cooperate with the Viet Cong, and in return the commander of the prison camp promised that he would let him go, as he had done for a few others in the past.

And so the tough young Marine became a model prisoner, even leading the camp's thought-reform group. His health remained relatively good for two years. But over time it gradually became clear that the commander had lied. He actually had no intention of releasing him. According to writer Doug Colligan's account of the incident, this is what happened next:

> When the full realization of this took hold, the soldier became a zombie. He refused to do all work, rejected all offers of food and encouragement, and simply lay on his cot, sucking his thumb. In a matter of weeks, he was dead.

If his cause of death could be summarized in one word, it would probably be: *hopelessness*.

You see, hopelessness can kill. In World War II, Korea, and Vietnam, doctors said many prisoners died from a condition they termed "give-up-itis." Facing grim conditions with no apparent prospect of freedom, some of the prisoners became demoralized and stuck in despair. With their hope drained, they slowly wasted away.

There's no question about it: The human spirit needs hope to survive and thrive. "Since my early years as a physician," wrote Dr. Arnold Hutschnecker, "I learned that taking away hope is, to most people, like pronouncing a death sentence. Their already hard-pressed will to live can be paralyzed, and they may give up and die."

Think of the horror of hopelessness. As I was reading a newspaper recently, I came across an article about a judge who sentenced a nineteen-year-old murderer to life in prison, with no possibility of parole.

Can you imagine that? No hope for freedom. It reminded me of the inscription over the entrance to hell in Dante's *Divine Comedy:* "All hope abandon, ye who enter here!"

The God of Hope

As I grappled with the question of what Jesus might say to the famous—and, in some cases, infamous—individuals profiled in this book, my mind kept coming back to the issue of what He would say to everyday people like you and me. What would He talk about if He came face-to-face with you? What words would He choose as you stood there staring Him in the eyes?

Somehow I think He would touch on the topic of hope. After all, the writers of the Bible recognized centuries ago that hope is central to the human spirit. "Hope deferred makes the heart sick," King Solomon wrote in Proverbs 13:12, "but a longing fulfilled is a tree of life."

In fact, the Bible could be called a book of hope. All told, there are eighty-six references to hope in the Old Testament, with another eighty in the New Testament. Hope is a theme that's woven throughout Scripture.

158

And in these days when your future may be uncertain—where your health may be precarious, where a sense of guilt may weigh you down, where the soaring crime rate punctuates life with a question mark and the environment is deteriorating, where people are increasingly alienated from each other, and where spirituality has become superficial—I think Jesus would tenderly put His arm around your shoulder and say: "I can understand your fears and frustrations, your anxieties and longings, but it's very important that you understand this about Me—*I am the God of hope.*"

Isn't that what the world wants? "People in many nations appear to be searching with a new intensity for spiritual moorings," wrote George Gallup, who has his finger on the public's pulse. "One of the key factors prompting this search is certainly a need for hope in these troubled times."

I believe Jesus would tell you, "I *am* that hope, because I'm the God of the second chance." He is uniquely capable of replenishing the hope that the world can sap from us. As the apostle Paul prayed in Romans 15:13: "May the God of hope fill you with all joy and peace as you trust in him, so that you may overflow with hope by the power of the Holy Spirit."

What Hope Isn't

God's hope, however, is different from what you might expect. We use the word *hope* all the time to mean different things. In fact, much of what we call *hope* could fall into three categories—wishful thinking, blind optimism, and personal dreams.

Wishful thinking is when we try to hope things in or out of existence. It's when we blow out the candles on our birthday cake and say to ourselves, "I hope I stay healthy for another year." It's when we pick up the *Wall Street Journal* and say, "I hope the prime rate drops again." It's when spring training begins and we say, "I hope the Cubs don't disappoint me again this year." (Hey, hope springs eternal!)

Wishful thinking is a kind of hopeful feeling that maybe, somehow, some way, things will go the way we want them to, even though we really don't have any power whatsoever to make it happen.

159

Another kind of hopeful attitude is blind optimism, like the guy who fell off a thirty-story building and yelled out as he passed the fifteenth floor, "Well, so far, so good!"

While it's good to have a generally optimistic outlook, some optimists see everything through rose-colored glasses. They paper over their problems as if they didn't exist. They avert their eyes from the ugly aspects of the world. To them, everything's just fine all the time—never mind the facts.

It's like the joke about the parents of two young twins. One of the boys was a depressed pessimist; the other was an incessant optimist. The parents were getting worried because each child's personality was becoming increasingly extreme. So just before Christmas, the father said, "We need to do something to break them out of their molds."

The parents decided to put dozens and dozens of shiny new toys in the pessimist's room, and to fill the optimist's room with piles of horse manure, hoping this would change their attitudes.

The children went to their rooms for a couple of hours, and then the pessimist came out. "Did you play with your new toys?" the father asked eagerly.

"Nah," moaned the pessimist. "I never even opened the packages. I was afraid that if I touched them, they'd just break, and then I'd be disappointed."

That's when the optimist came bounding out of his room that had been filled with horse manure. He was all smiles. "How come you're so happy?" asked the dad.

The little boy beamed and said, "I just know that if I keep digging long enough, *I'm going to find the pony!*"

Do you know people like that—optimists who pretend everything's always great and who gloss over problems in their lives?

And then there's hope that takes the form of personal dreams. These are the lofty goals we set for our lives and which we work so hard to achieve. In other words we don't just hope for a new car, but we begin saving for one. We don't just hope we'll become a better golfer, but we take lessons and spend time on the practice tee. We don't just wish for good health, but we begin to watch our diet and participate in an exercise program.

Generally, there's nothing wrong with that. But problems arise when our personal dreams are restricted by our own limitations or when they fall victim to factors beyond our control.

For instance, I suppose a lot of General Motors workers had personal dreams of job security and retirement, but that didn't stop GM from announcing one day that they were going to eliminate thousands of employees. Unfortunately our dreams are often at the mercy of others.

Anchoring Our Hope

Biblical hope is different. For most people, hoping is something that they *do*, but the Bible talks about hope as something they can *possess*. We can actually grab hold of it. For someone who follows Jesus, hope is the secure expectation that He is both willing and able to make good on the promises He has made to us.

The Bible refers to this as "living hope," because it's linked directly to the resurrection of Christ. The apostle Peter wrote in 1 Peter 1:3–4: "In [God's] great mercy he has given us new birth into a living hope through the resurrection of Jesus Christ from the dead, and into an inheritance that can never perish, spoil or fade—kept in heaven for you."

You see, through His decisive conquest of death, Jesus demonstrated that He really is God and that He really does have the power to fulfill His promises in the pages of Scripture. Promises to change our lives. Promises to guide us. Promises that He'll cause good to emerge from our personal difficulties. Promises that His followers will spend eternity with Him.

"We have this hope as an anchor for the soul, firm and secure," says Hebrews 6:19. Usually I hate to use sailing analogies because I can get seasick drinking a glass of water, but an anchor is a great metaphor. Our hope is only as good as what we anchor it to.

Let's face it: In and of itself, hope doesn't have any power to change reality. We hope for this, we hope for that, and we might feel better for a while. We may even fool ourselves into thinking everything's okay. But the only way hope has any real power is when we anchor it to the God who has real power. And not only real power, but a heartfelt desire to help.

161

And I think Jesus would say to you, "Whatever you're facing, I can infuse hope into your life—a hope that's firm and secure. In fact, let Me describe for you two specific ways I can introduce hope to you—by absolving you of your past, and by assuring you of your future."

Absolving Our Past

"This I call to mind and therefore I have hope," the prophet Jeremiah wrote in Lamentations 3:21–23. "Because of the LORD's great love we are not consumed, for his compassions never fail. They are new every morning; great is your faithfulness."

The writer is saying that we can live with hope because even though we find ourselves failing God, letting down our families, and even falling short of our own expectations, God's forgiveness is a renewable resource. It's fresh and available every day, and He's willing to offer us a new start.

I was thinking about this while I was watching the movie *City Slickers*. Did you see that film? It was about three New Yorkers who were approaching their midlife crises, and they decided to take an adventure vacation during which they participated in a cattle drive out West.

Phil's life was a wreck. He was in a dead-end job at his father-in-law's grocery store and he was facing a divorce. In one scene he and his buddies were in a tent when Phil broke down and began crying. "I'm at a dead end!" he sobbed. "I'm almost forty years old; I've wasted my life!"

One of his friends tried to console him. "But now you've got a chance to start over," he said. "Remember when we were kids and we'd be playing ball and the ball would get stuck up in a tree or something? We'd yell, '*Do over!*' Look, Phil—your life is a do-over. You've got a clean slate!"

But Phil wasn't so sure. "I've got no place to live. I'm going to get wiped out in the divorce because I've committed adultery, so I may never see my kids again. I'm alone!" he said. "How's that slate look now?"

As I watched that scene, I thought, *How is a guy like Phil ever really going to be helped?* And the answer is only through the kind of do-over that he can get from God. After all, God is the world's biggest dispenser of do-overs. He *loves* granting them to contrite and humble recipients.

Individuals like Phil—and you and I—can wish we'd never committed the wrongs we have. We can try to paper them over like they never really happened. We can try to deal with them on our own. But Jesus Christ would tell us, "I can erase them so you can start over. I can forgive you, and I can help you heal and hope again."

Squeezing Out Hope

Some people need a do-over from God because guilt has been squeezing the hope out of their lives. That was the case with a woman who wrote to me about the turbulence in her life.

She explained that several years ago she had been living with her boyfriend when she got pregnant. Even though she wanted the baby very much, her controlling and domineering boyfriend talked her into having an abortion. Later he abandoned her.

"For years, I was miserable," the woman wrote. "I was ashamed of myself for not being strong enough to stand up for myself or for my baby."

That's what guilt does. It tries to convince us that our wrongdoing disqualifies us from ever starting over. Guilt robs us of hope. It tells us we're not just people who have failed, but that we're failures as people and therefore beyond redemption.

A stifling sense of remorse haunted this young woman until she didn't know where to turn. Finally, in desperation, she turned to Jesus Christ and implored Him for a do-over. And what happened amazed her—He not only forgave her and wiped her slate clean, but He helped her through the process of healing her emotions as well.

Now that God has renewed her sense of hope, it's like the darkness has lifted and a new day has dawned. Just before she was baptized as a new follower of Jesus, she wrote: "I can't thank God enough for all the grace I have received from Him."

I had the privilege of baptizing her in front of a crowd of several thousand people. By her participation in that sacrament, she was declaring to the world that this God who gave her a new beginning is the God she wants to follow forever.

And if your own life is weighted down with guilt—shame over a marriage that went bad, or kids who've gone astray, or promises to God that you've broken—then maybe it's time for you to ask Jesus Christ for a do-over.

The question isn't, "Will He give me one?" The issue isn't, "Does the magnitude of my wrongdoing make me ineligible?" The extent of your foul-ups has never been an impediment. Romans 5:20 says, "Where sin increased, grace increased all the more."

Jesus Christ has publicly declared Himself ready, willing, and able to grant you a do-over; the real issue is whether you have the humility to ask Him for one.

God of the Second Chance

Then there are those people who can relate to Phil in *City Slickers* because they're coming to realize, like him, that they've been wasting their lives in a lot of ways. They've pursued their hopes and dreams long enough to accumulate a bunch of stuff that, in the end, has failed to satisfy their soul.

Like the successful executive who sat across from me at lunch and told me how empty he felt despite all he had achieved in business. Now, there was nothing wrong with his accomplishments, which were quite impressive.

But he said to me: "I've been a casual Christian all my life, and I'm sick to death of it." He almost spit out the words in disgust. "It's a boring and frustrating life, and I want to stop, but I don't know what to do. I feel like I've blown my chance and let too many years go by."

I'll tell you what I told him: It's never too late for a do-over. It's never too late to say to God, "I don't want to squander my life anymore. Let me start over, and this time, with the help of Your Holy Spirit, I'll do my best to keep my compass pointed in Your direction. I want to experience the excitement of being a fully devoted follower of Christ. I want to feel the thrill of pursuing a mission in life that really matters. I want my life to add up to something more than just a bunch of disposable stuff."

God absolutely *revels* in answering those prayers! If you feel like you've missed the Christian adventure, take heart—there's hope in the God of the second chance.

Assuring Our Future

Not only is there hope because Jesus Christ can absolve us of our past, but we have access to the ultimate hope of heaven because He has the power to assure us of a future in eternity with Him. That can help us maintain our hopefulness even in a world that's plagued by danger and death.

"Whether or not we admit it to ourselves, we are all haunted by a truly awful sense of impermanence," wrote playwright Tennessee Williams. "Fear and evasion are the two little beasts that chase each other's tails in the revolving wire cage of our nervous world."

I can remember the days when I didn't believe there was a God. Sometimes I'd lie awake at night, staring into the darkness, and think about the hopelessness of life. I was convinced that when a person dies, that's it. There's nothing more. Nearly one out of six Americans believes that, and that's a depressing formula for hopelessness. Said Woody Allen: "You have to deny the reality of death to go on every day."

Some people try to cope through wishful thinking: "Maybe when I die, I'll be reincarnated or something." Or they engage in blind optimism: "I just won't think about it. By the time I get around to dying, they'll have a cure for whatever I've got." Others pursue personal dreams: "I'll cut my weight, I'll trim my fat intake, I'll reduce my cholesterol, and I'll be able to lengthen my life span."

These defense mechanisms may make people feel better for a while, but they don't change the reality that death plays a perfect game: One out of one dies. And the tricky thing is that death has a particularly annoying tendency to be unpredictable.

I was talking about that one day with a computer salesman named Jeff Miller, who lives near me in suburban Chicago. He was telling me about a fateful United Airlines flight he took in 1989, when he was traveling home from Colorado Springs.

While he was reading a paperback, there was a muffled explosion on the DC-10. The jetliner swayed to the side so violently that he dropped his book in the aisle. As it turned out, the engine in the plane's tail had exploded, crippling the jet's steering mechanism.

Over the next several minutes, as the jumbo airliner lumbered toward an emergency landing at Sioux City, Iowa, it became clear that the situation was desperate. Some passengers began shaking; others sobbed from fear. A few put on a face of optimism and kept insisting there was nothing to worry about. And Jeff—who has been a Christian for several years—spent the time quietly praying a simple prayer that was anchored in hope.

"Thank You, Lord, that You're mine and I'm Yours," he whispered. "God, I want to live. But I know if I don't, I'll be with You, and You'll care for my family."

You see, Jeff had a secure expectation that God would fulfill His promises.

The Edge of Eternity

Do you remember seeing the news footage of that plane when it cartwheeled onto the runway and exploded into orange flames? Jeff braced himself for a violent death, but it never came. His piece of the fuselage broke off and tumbled into a cornfield, where he found himself upside down, still strapped into his seat, not a mark on him.

I asked Jeff, "What was it like when everybody realized that the plane was going down? I mean, people don't usually survive airplane crashes. Was there a sense of hopelessness among the passengers?"

"Lee, I'll tell you the truth—it was scary," Jeff replied. "But at the same time, I felt like I was full of hope. There was hope if I lived, and there was the hope that if I died, I'd be with Christ. It's like it says in the Psalms—what can anybody do to you if your hope is in the Lord?"

Jeff wasn't the only passenger to feel that way. Helen Young Hayes, a securities analyst from Denver, told *Life* magazine: "After the flight attendant explained the emergency landing procedures, we were left with our thoughts. That's when I began praying. I closed my eyes and thought, *Dear Lord, I pray that You will guide the pilot's hands.*"

She described herself as being full of peace because she knew that whatever happened, she wasn't really facing the end. "There I was," she said, "sitting on the edge of eternity."

Isn't it true that how we face death says a lot about how we have faced life? The Bible says that because followers of Christ have the secure hope of spending eternity with Him, they can live with boldness and confidence and courage. My attitudes toward both death and life were turned upside down when I became a Christian, in ways that I'm still trying to fully understand.

For instance, a while ago—before she was thrust into the national limelight through the brutal attack on her—I was watching a television program about Olympic skater Nancy Kerrigan. The camera showed her beautiful and elegant performance on the ice, and then it panned to the side of the rink, where Nancy's mother, Brenda, had her nose nearly pressed against the screen of a large television set.

You see, Brenda had been stricken virtually blind when she was thirty-one years old, and she needed to get right up to the TV in order to see her daughter performing. The interviewer asked her what she was able to make out.

"Well," she said slowly, "I can see some shapes. And I can detect some color and movement when she jumps. . . ." Then, suddenly, she burst into tears, sobbing uncontrollably. After she caught her breath, she said: "But I can't see her face. I can't see my daughter's face!" And then she cried some more.

That poignant moment helped me understand something that I had been feeling, because it reminded me of my relationship with Jesus Christ. Increasingly over the years, I've been able to sense Him comforting me during difficult times. I've detected His presence and power in my life. I've felt Him gently guiding me and loving me and encouraging me. But as much as I want to, *I can't see His face.*

And yet I have the secure hope that someday I'll stand before Him and look squarely into His eyes. For those who know Him as their personal forgiver, that's not something to fear; it's something to anticipate with great excitement. God has liberated me from a state of hopelessness, and now I have a future that's bursting with expectation!

So let me ask you this: What better step can you take than to say, "I want to be absolved of my past and assured of my future. I want a hope that's not based on wishful thinking or blind optimism or my own personal dreams, but which is anchored in the actual historical event of the resurrection of Jesus Christ."

I think—no, I *know*—that Jesus would tell you, "That hope is yours whenever you want to receive it."

Just Say the Name

Earlier I described a soldier whose descent into hopelessness eventually drained the life out of him. Now I want to conclude with a story about another prisoner—someone who discovered firsthand the hope that comes when Jesus Christ absolves our past and assures our future.

Bob McAlister, at the time the deputy chief of staff for the governor of South Carolina, became a volunteer for Prison Fellowship after he became a Christian. In an article for *Jubilee* magazine, he described how he was visiting Death Row in a prison in Columbia, South Carolina, when he saw a stomach-churning sight in a cell occupied by Ronald "Rusty" Woomer.

"Rusty, his face the color of chalk, was sitting on the floor—motionless," Bob wrote. "Crawling aimlessly like so many drunks, dozens of roaches covered the walls and floor. But what froze my soul were the roaches crawling on the man—his lap, his shoulders—and such was his despair that he did not flick them off."

This thirty-five-year-old murderer of four innocent people, who was facing the inevitability of the electric chair, had sunk to the depths of hopelessness, careening down the same dead-end road as that young Marine in Vietnam.

Bob wasn't sure how to react to this depressing scene. Finally, he pleaded: "Rusty, just say the name *Jesus*." Slowly and painfully, with all the effort he could muster, the nearly comatose inmate whispered the name of the Savior of the world.

And then Bob began to explain to him how Jesus is the God of hope. It was clear that Rusty was paying attention. At the end, when Bob asked if he wanted to accept Christ's offer of forgiveness, Rusty nodded. Through his tears, he prayed: "Jesus, I've hurt a lot of people. Ain't no way that I deserve You to hear me. But I'm tired and I'm sick and I'm lonely. My mama's died and she's in heaven with You, and I never got to tell her bye. Please forgive me, Jesus, for everything I've done. I don't know much about You, but I'm willin' to learn, and I thank You for listenin' to me."

God's Majestic Assurance

Bob returned the following week. "I walked up to his cell; it was spotless," he recalled. "Gone were the dirt and roaches and porno magazines. The walls were scrubbed, the bed was made, and the scent of disinfectant hung in the air."

Rusty was smiling and enthusiastic. "Bob, how do you like it?" he asked. "I spent all weekend cleaning out my cell 'cause I figured that's what Jesus wanted me to do."

Over the next four and a half years, Rusty and Bob became close friends, the kind the Bible describes as being knit together at the soul. They read the Scriptures together. They talked and listened to each other. They prayed.

Rusty described a childhood of poverty and abuse. By the time he was a teenager, he was living in public rest rooms and under bridges. His only fond memories of his childhood were of going fishing with his mother, a woman who lived a deprived and difficult life. At the time she died, Rusty was devastated but relieved. "I knew," he said, "that nothing could ever hurt her or do bad things to her again."

She even influenced his thoughts about eternity. Sometimes he'd talk about it during those long hours with Bob. "When I get to heaven," he'd muse, "Jesus and my mama are gonna be waitin' for me. And my mama and me are gonna go fishin'."

Rusty didn't try to rationalize his crimes. He accepted responsibility for what he had done and felt deeply remorseful over the pain he had caused. "If my death will bring peace to the people I've hurt so bad, then it's time for me to die," he said.

Amazingly he received a letter from the younger brother of one of his victims, graciously offering forgiveness. Lee Hewitt, who was a Christian, explained: "Rusty and I are now brothers in Christ, and I had no choice but to forgive him."

At one point Lee visited him in a tearful encounter at the prison. "What you have done is make God's Word complete for me," Rusty told him. In a way, Bob explained, Lee's forgiveness embodied the forgiveness Rusty had received from Christ.

Over time, one by one, the courts turned down Rusty's appeals. His execution ticked closer. It was clear that wishful thinking and blind optimism and personal dreams were useless. All Rusty had left was the hope of Christ. And yet that was what he needed the most.

Finally, the day of his execution arrived. "As we sat there the peace of God washed over us both—a peace that I cannot begin to describe," Bob wrote. "In that darkened, quiet cell after a frenetic day of emotional upheaval, God chose to move in our hearts, replacing the burdens and fears with the majestic assurance that Rusty would break away from the body of sin and suffering and be whisked away to heaven."

Less than an hour before his electrocution, Rusty was taken to the prison barber so his head and right leg could be shaved. "Paps," as he called his friend Bob, "read me the Bible one last time."

Bob opened his Bible to the comforting words of Revelation 21:4, "He will wipe every tear from their eyes," the passage says. "There will be no more death or mourning or crying or pain."

"Rusty was smiling—a peaceful smile that I have never seen on another human being," Bob recalled. "I do not know his thoughts, but they were the thoughts of a man who was not afraid of death."

Here's Bob's description of what happened next:

> At 12:55 A.M., they came to get him. After reading him the death warrant, Warden George Martin asked, "Rusty, are you ready?"
>
> "Let's go," he replied.
>
> I followed Rusty to the death chamber, and my final words to him were, "Rusty, look to Jesus."
>
> Rusty was strapped into the chair, a leather strap over his right leg and a leather helmet attached to his head. I heard his last words: "I'm sorry. I claim Jesus Christ as my Savior. My only wish is that everyone in the world could feel the love I have felt from Him."

Rusty's body died at 1:05 A.M. But I am convinced that he and his mama are fishin' in heavenly streams.

Our Hope of Heaven

You might read Rusty's story and say to yourself, "Well, he really *needed* Jesus. He was a cold-blooded killer. But me—c'mon, I've never killed anybody."

Yet the Bible stresses that all of us are in a hopeless situation. We've all violated God's laws in one way or the other. In fact, Jesus said that God's greatest law is to love Him with all of our heart, soul, mind, and strength, and to love our neighbor as ourselves. Certainly we've all fallen short of that.

And just as we prescribe the highest penalties for people who violate society's greatest laws, God's justice demands that we suffer His ultimate penalty—being separated from Him for all eternity in a place of utter hopelessness.

God has no choice but to be an honest judge and declare us guilty. He can't pretend we're innocent because that would be a lie. That's the predicament we face, and no amount of wishful thinking or blind optimism or personal dreaming can change it.

But Jesus can. Because you matter so much to Him, Jesus Christ willingly stepped forward to suffer the death penalty as your substitute so that you could be absolved of your past and assured of your future. And, friends, that's the only reason we can have hope.

What would Jesus say to you? I could imagine Him saying: "The choice is yours. You can pay the penalty for your wrongdoing, or you can accept My payment on your behalf, just like Rusty did. You need to know this: *The hope of heaven is yours for the asking.*"

It's my prayer that with a heart of repentance and faith, you'll just say the name *Jesus*.

In fact, let me conclude with a prayer for you. The words belong to the apostle Paul, who wrote them in a letter to the Ephesians, as translated by J. B. Phillips:

> This is my prayer. That the God of our Lord Jesus
> Christ, the all-glorious Father, will give you spiritual wis-
> dom and the insight to know more of him: that you may

receive that inner illumination of the spirit which will make you realize how great is the hope to which he is calling you—the magnificence and splendor of the inheritance promised to Christians—and how tremendous is the power available to us who believe in God.

That power is the same divine energy which was demonstrated in Christ when he raised him from the dead and gave him the place of highest honor in Heaven—a place that is infinitely superior to any command, authority, power or control, and which carries with it a name far beyond any name that could ever be used in this world or the world to come.